A FIGHTING CHANCE

THE SAGA CONTINUES

BOOK 2

A FIGHTING CHANCE

THE SAGA CONTINUES

BOOK 2

BY
JOE MANNO

You can do anything! Never give up! God Bless You

 RTC ENTERTAINMENT INC

REACHING THE CHILDREN

A FIGHTING CHANCE
The Saga Continues
Book 2

by Joe Manno

RTC ENTERTAINMENT INC

REACHING THE CHILDREN

© 2003 RTC Entertainment, Inc.
P.O. Box 609138
Orlando, Florida 32860-9138
www.rtcentertainment.com

Cover Design by Aimee Vargas
Illustrations by Jonathan Charles Vaughan

International Standard Book Number: 0-97185-012-7

Published in the United States of America
03 04 05 06 07 08 — 9 8 7 6 5 4 3 2 1

A wise man discerns the consequences before he takes action.

—Joe Manno

A FIGHTING CHANCE

The saga continues...
   Are you ready for some unforgettable zany
adventures? It is time to discover what happens when you
add amazing technology, power rings, peer pressure,
talents and competition to everyday life. You actually have
A FIGHTING CHANCE!

   Learn how Mr. Galardi's mishap taught him more
about himself than he ever knew before. See how a pushy
karate teacher finally helps his son follow his own dream.
Does competition have a place for friendship? Can a gang
of delinquents possibly do the next right thing?

   In the pages of this book you will find nail-
biting suspense, great giggle-humor, and heart-melting
revelations. You might even see yourself!.

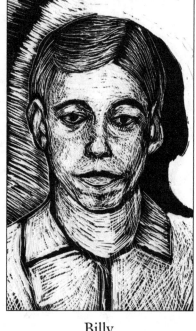

Adam

Billy

D.J.

Dominique

Jackie

Josh

Kelly

Yuri

A FIGHTING CHANCE BOOK 2
The Saga Continues

Chapter
One

The Adventure Continues

Mr. Gunner, who is really Mr. Galardi, had just walked out of the school on a Saturday morning after meeting with Miss Ward, Mrs. Rossenheimer, Mr. Edwards and the superintendent. Once everything was ironed out with the teachers, Joseph Galardi, also known as Mr. Gunner, entered the transport door from the parking lot of the school. That's when everything went haywire.

Back at the Zone, his team had been monitoring his location. Adam, Josh, Billy, DJ, Dominique, Jackie, Yuri and Kelly were at their workstations. All of a sudden, the red light started to flash, and an alarm began to sound. Everyone worked frantically to give Adam every readout he asked for.

Another alarm sounded, and then two more went off at the same time. Adam ran to the large map that had been titled the "Joe Locator."

Adam quickly tried to pinpoint Mr. Galardi's whereabouts when both alarms suddenly stopped. The entire team froze. Everyone stared at Adam, but he didn't move a muscle. There was silence. Coldness filled the room.

Dominique broke the silence, "Adam, where's my dad?"

He slowly turned his head toward Dominique and answered quietly, "I don't know."

Feeling the intense pressure, Adam began to react in the search for Mr. Galardi. "Kelly, give me the temperature reading one hundred miles above the earth's service. The code is 12759-DAC, David, Apple, Charley. Josh, hand me that empty can of orange juice. Billy, pull all three of my files marked 'Print Retrieve.' Jackie, there is a can right there behind you with a small brush attached to it. Please bring that to me."

Adam looked over at Dominique and saw her in a state of shock while tears rolled down her face. "I will find your dad! Don't you worry about a thing. Do you see that red light blinking on the upper right hand side of my computer? That's the pulse sensor in your dad's watch; it indicates that he's alive. The transmitter part of the watch seems to have been damaged because there's no response by radio. His pulse is sixty-four beats per minute."

"Is that good?" Dominique asked with great concern.

"It's good if he's sleeping," Adam replied, knowing that something was not right. He quickly changed the subject. "Kelly, the temperature, please."

"Adam, I don't have a temperature reading. My screen says XJ743. What does that mean?"

"That means it's very cold up there, which is exactly what we need for this laser wave to work properly. If the temperature is too warm, the laser wave will give us an improper reading."

Not even explaining what the temperature reading meant, Adam quickly exploded with two different thoughts. "Jackie, the can and brush, please. Billy, copy each disk to my laptop and let me know when you are done."

Billy responded immediately to Adam's request, while Jackie handed Adam the can and brush. "What's this for?"

"Open the can for me and watch," Adam replied, as he took the brush. He dipped it into the can of powder, grabbed the empty can of orange juice and moved the brush several times over the can.

"What are you doing?" DJ asked, totally confused.

Out of nowhere, Josh spoke, "Prints."

DJ gave Josh a goofy stare before responding to his remark. "What do you mean, 'prints'?"

"Fingerprints," Josh replied. "He's looking for Mr. Galardi's fingerprints on the can."

"And there they are," Adam announced, smiling.

"What are you going to do with my dad's fingerprints?" asked Dominique.

A beep went off from Adam's laptop, which quickly drew his attention in that direction.

"What does that mean?" Jackie quickly questioned.

"That's not good," Adam replied, as he peered at the monitor. "His pulse rate is dropping. It's fifty-four beats per minute, and that's too low for an active heart rate." Adam tapped his finger on the desk, pondering what he was certain was fact.

"What's happening, Adam?" Dominique said with a panicky tone in her voice. "You're scaring me."

Noticing Dominique's response, Adam took a moment to gather the proper words so she wouldn't freak out. He looked at her, but his hesitation made her more nervous and concerned. Not finding any easy way to tell her, he just came right out with it. "He's unconscious. I know he is." Adam spoke with great concern.

Dominique began to panic. "Oh my gosh! Do something, Adam!"

Adam looked over at Billy, not saying a word. Billy quickly responded to Adam, "Just tell me what you need me to do."

Adam replied with great seriousness. "The watch is operated by a satellite remote radio magnetic shock wave…" Adam paused for a moment and took a deep breath. "I want you to initiate a Level Four shock wave to the watch. If it works, the watch will send a jolt of electricity into Mr. Galardi. I hope it will help him regain consciousness. However, there is one set back. Within ten seconds of this happening, the watch will be totally destroyed. It was not meant to handle that much power, which means…"

Yuri cut him off, saying, "We will lose any hope of contact with him."

"Is that true, Adam?" Dominique asked.

Before Adam could answer, Josh answered the question. "We have already lost contact with him. We have ten seconds to read the screen to find out if his pulse rate goes up or not. If it goes up, that means he has regained consciousness."

Billy waited at the computer. "I'm ready, Adam. Give me the code."

"You already know the code, Billy." Adam replied. "Just reengage the shock wave program and increase its arrival point to Level Four."

Billy moved his fingers quickly across the keypad as he entered the code to initiate the shock wave. Within a few seconds Billy stopped typing and put his finger on the return key, indicating that he was ready to push the button. He looked up at Adam for the go ahead.

"Kelly, I want you to print this out just in case we forget what we see. That will allow us to go back and study the results." Adam paused for a moment. "Is everyone ready?"

He received nods from the team. He looked over at Billy and gave him a nod to go ahead.

Billy hesitated a second, then pushed the button. The process had begun.

"There it is," Adam said. "The computer is showing that the shock wave is transmitting. This is going to work. Kelly, begin printing these readouts. Here we go. We have ten seconds from right...now. His pulse rate is still at fifty-four beats per minute. Any second we should see this number begin to climb."

Another red light began to blink on the opposite side of the screen.

"Not good," Adam said with concern in his voice. He studied the screen with great intent, and without warning he yelled, "No!" as he pounded his hand onto the desktop. His reaction scared the team half to death. "We lost transmission. We have no way of knowing if the electrical shock worked or not."

"Now what?" Billy questioned, ready to do whatever Adam needed from him.

Dominique put her head in her hands. "I can't take this any more. I have to call my mother. She needs to know what happened."

"Just wait." Adam requested. "Let me gather more information. I told you that I'll find your father, and I will. The machine did not falter. Everything went as planned. I just don't know what happened on the other end when the door opened."

Adam stayed silent for a moment, allowing Dominique to digest everything he just said.

With her head still resting in her hands, Dominique

gathered her thoughts and pulled her emotions together. Expressing a professional and mature attitude, she lifted her head and acknowledged that Adam was right. "Do whatever you need to do."

Chapter
Two

The Search for Mr. Galardi

Kelly, has there been any temperature change?" Adam asked, getting back to business.

"Everything is still the same. I need to ask you a question," Kelly said, curiously. "Can you explain this temp thing to me and why you need Mr. Galardi's fingerprints off an empty orange juice can?"

"No! I mean yes, of course. The prints are going to help me find Mr. Galardi. This is one of my favorite inventions. Let's just keep going. I'll show you how it works as we go."

Adam reached for the orange juice can and a roll of masking tape.

Just to the right of the laptop sat a small digital camera, about the size of a quarter. Adam began to describe what was going to happen.

"With this small camera, this roll of masking tape, Kelly's temperature reading and the three programs Billy just installed on my computer—by the way, are they ready?

"Ready and waiting, boss." Billy answered.

"Good," Adam responded. He continued, "We will

not only locate Mr. Galardi, but we'll be able to see him as well."

"I gotta see this," DJ said, crossing his arms.

"Still questioning my abilities, huh, DJ?"

"No! I mean...I'm just excited to see the whole thing work and to see Mr. Galardi be safe and stuff...well, a little, I guess."

Adam did not even try to defend himself. He was the kind of person who proved his abilities through his actions, not a lot of words. Adam began to tape the can and explained as he went.

"I have to tape off a small square to define the exact area of contact so that the camera can pick up a precise copy of the fingerprint. The computer will transform it into a molecular structure, defining its complete DNA readout so that it can be downloaded onto my laptop. Then it will be transported to a satellite. That's why the temperature cannot rise above a certain degree or else it will not transport properly. That's a long story. I'll save it for another time, so let's just keep going. Once the satellite receives and processes the print, it will use a high powered magnetic laser, blanketing every human that exists on this planet until it finds the exact match. Once the search is complete, we can upload our requests—in this case, a photograph. I'm working on a live video feed, but it's not ready at this time."

"I actually understood everything you just said," Jackie said proudly.

DJ thought of a question to ask, but hesitated. Then he decided he just couldn't hold back any longer. "Is it really going to work? I mean, how do you figure these things out?"

Adam smiled, as even he realized that his plan must be hard to comprehend. "This is my gift. This is how my brain works. It comes simply to me, just like sports comes easy to you. To answer your other question, 'Will it work'? Not only will it work, but we also will have all our information within thirty seconds."

"That's my man. I taught him everything he knows," Billy said with a smile on his face.

Kelly just looked at him and shook her head. "You are such a dork."

Billy shot right back, "Call me what you want, but I get to work the computer."

"You really mean it? I can call you whatever I want?" Kelly responded.

Billy was reluctant to answer the question for fear of what might come out of Kelly's mouth. "Is it going to be nice?"

"What do you think?" Kelly answered.

Before Billy could answer, Adam cut in on the little cat-and-mouse game. "I think we should get back to work and find our fearless leader...if that's OK with you two."

"I think that's a great idea," Billy said, smiling at Kelly.

Kelly gave him a "whatever" look to express how immature she thought Billy was acting.

It was obvious that Billy liked Kelly, but whenever he tried to communicate with her it came out all wrong. The look on his face showed that he was thinking through every word he had just spoken as he tried to figure out where he went wrong and why Kelly had not responded in a more positive way. After a moment, he shook it off and focused on the computer screen, awaiting Adam's next request.

Josh got up from his chair and made his way over to the empty orange juice can. He picked up the can and placed it in front of the camera, about two inches from the lens. "Is this too close?" Josh asked Adam.

Before Adam could respond, Jackie questioned Josh's aggression. "What are you doing?"

Josh responded in a very calm and polite voice, "Too much talk and not enough effort to find our friend."

Silence overtook the room as the team realized that focus was needed if they were going to pull this off. No one spoke. However, the mood had changed, and everyone concentrated on the seriousness of the problem.

Adam looked around the room and then back at Josh. "Actually, yes, it's too close. It needs to be at least four inches away from the lens."

Josh adjusted the can, bringing it to Adam's exact specifications.

"Billy, listen closely," Adam said, as he immediately directed another order to Kelly. "Again, Kelly, we will need to copy our tracks so we can look back on them later if necessary.

"Got it," Kelly responded as she began to program her keypad computer that she wore around her waist.

Adam continued his instructions to Billy. "Billy, the three programs you installed are geared to respond one after the other. Once you activate the process, you will

11

need to keep a close eye on the computer screen. When the green light flashes, you need to key in confirmation in order to move to the next program. Once you have gone through all three programs, a red light will blink. The red light shows that the process has been completed, and within ten seconds our subject will be located."

Adam looked right at Dominique. "In this case, 'subject located' means that your dad has been found."

She smiled, showing that Adam's words somewhat comforted her, but she was aware that there was a lot that had to be done before she could breathe a sigh of relief.

"Are you ready, Billy?" Adam asked, ready to begin the process.

"Ready!"

"Activate Program One," Adam instructed.

Billy keyed the numbers. "Program One, activated."

The intensity in and around the mill was so great that no one could take their eyes off the screen even though they really didn't know what they were looking for.

Suddenly, a beeping noise sounded.

"What's that?" Dominique asked fearfully.

"Relax." Adam said calmly. "It's just the green light I was talking about. It signals Billy to confirm the transaction to the next program."

Adam looked around the room and saw that everyone was just looking back at him.

"Sorry, I forgot to tell you about the beeping noise."

"Program Two has been activated," Billy said as he concentrated.

DJ slouched in his chair with his arms crossed and an

intense look frozen on his face. His eyebrows were tightly pulled together; his lips pressed firmly against one another. It looked as if he wasn't even breathing

Billy signaled, "Program three has been activated."

Yuri concentrated on the screen with such intensity that his ever familiar smile seemed to be frozen on his face. Nothing was funny, that's just what happens when Yuri gets nervous.

"Adam, the red light is blinking, but is that beeping sound supposed to be happening?" Billy asked with concern.

"No the beeping is not supposed to be happening," Adam replied.

"What's the matter?" Dominique asked fearfully.

DJ unfolded his arms and moved closer to the screen. "What does that mean, Adam?"

"It means that Kelly is standing on the cable cord, and the computer is alerting us to get off." Adam said, pleased to deliver good news this time.

Kelly jumped off the cord and looked around at all the others. "Oops!"

Attention was taken off Kelly when Adam quickly responded to the latest activity on the screen.

"Here it comes...Any second now...Bingo! There he is—right where we programmed him in the first place. One block north of the Navy Peer in Chicago, Illinois. Billy, punch in C, comma, 432."

Billy responded immediately to Adam's request. "Done."

Adam looked intently at the screen. "Keep your eyes

on the screen and watch this."

DJ, still a little reluctant, watched along with the rest of them.

Adam commented. "Smile, Mr. Galardi, we're about to take your picture."

The Fighting Chance team awaited the transmission with smiles of hope on each of them. Within a few seconds the smiles disappeared, and shock and concern overtook their faces.

"Is that my dad?" Dominique asked, not happy with what she saw.

"Billy, hit the F5 key to zoom in on the picture." Adam said, not taking his eyes off the screen.

Billy reacted immediately, and the picture zoomed in within a matter of seconds.

"What happened to him?" Yuri said, without his characteristic smile.

"I don't know. Give me a second, please," Adam replied as he looked closer to study the picture.

Mr. Galardi was on the ground, resting on his left elbow. He looked as if he had just pulled his hand away from his eyebrow, and it was filled with either blood or dirt.

"I can't tell whether he has dirt on his face and hands or if it is..."

Dominique cut him off, "Don't say it, Adam, please."

"Billy, hit shift, hold it down and then the F7 key. I need the picture to be in color. As soon as you are done with that, hit the F15 key three times, and it will send us three consecutive pictures of his progress so we can see if he has gotten off the ground. Apparently the electric shock worked."

Billy responded to Adam's request, and the picture changed quickly to color.

As soon as Dominique could see that it was blood and not dirt, she let out a loud scream. The team freaked out, and Kelly reacted in the same manner, returning an even louder scream.

"Here you go, Adam. Look at these three pictures," Billy said waiting for Adam's response.

"He appears to be on his feet...or at least trying," Adam commented with a ray of hope.

"Now what?" Jackie asked, awaiting a positive answer.

Without answering the question, Adam looked closer at the screen.

"Billy, use the mouse and zoom in closer on this object laying on the ground."

Billy did as Adam requested.

"What is that?" Yuri asked with confusion.

"That's his cell phone," Josh said.

Before Adam could comment, Billy was already dialing. "It's ringing."

Everyone waits with anticipation. Dominique bites on her nail in hopes that her dad answers the phone and she can be at ease.

"It's going to his voice mail. Let me try again." Billy says.

"Wait a minute." Josh says with great concern as he continues. "Look at the next picture. Zoom in on his right foot."

Knowing exactly what to do, Billy maneuvers the keys and the picture came in clear. They could see the cell phone next to Mr. Galardi's right foot.

Josh's concern proved to be as he expected. "The

phone is destroyed. He must have stepped on it or something like that."

Dominique took a more positive attitude. "We just have to wait. He'll get to a phone, and he'll call us. I know he will. At least we know he's alive. Thank you for finding my dad, Adam. Thank you all."

On a lighter note, Billy sat back in his chair and stretched his arms out in front of him while putting his hands together and cracking his knuckles. With a proud look on his face he responded to Dominique's comment. "Dominique, finding your father is not a problem at all when you have the technology and talent that I have."

Jackie biffed Billy on the back of the head, while Yuri fired a piece of paper that hit him at the same time. Everyone laughed at the lighter moment of this hectic morning.

Kelly crossed her arms and shook her head while looking right at Billy. "You see what I mean. You are a dork, and you do this to yourself." Even though Kelly was somewhat joking, her comment, she felt, was quite appropriate and fitting for the moment.

Billy laughed along with everyone else, but the dork part did hurt his feelings. He felt he had failed again in winning Kelly's interest. Not one to dwell on the moment, he addressed the team.

"Enough about me. Let's man these phones. Mr. Galardi should be calling any minute.

Chapter Three

The Shocking News

Three hours passed, and still no call from Mr. Galardi. Early evening approached before the team contacted their families and told them that they were not going to leave the mill until they heard from Mr. Galardi…or at least figure out what was going on.

Mrs. Galardi came to the mill to bring the kids something to eat but her spirits weren't very high due to the present situation. She wasn't in tears because she had seen pictures of her husband up and alive. However, her concern along with the rest remained quite serious.

Adam had not taken his eyes off the computer for quite some time.

Several more pictures had been downloaded, and Mr. Galardi seemed to just be wandering around, not really going anywhere. One picture in particular had Adam concerned. Mr. Galardi was sitting on a bench with his head in his hands. He looked very confused.

"I'm concerned about this picture. Something looks wrong." Adam said, expressing his thought aloud.

The team gathered around to look for themselves and try to figure out what Adam was talking about.

"Maybe he's just resting," Yuri commented.

"I think we should call Captain Miller and let them handle this," Mrs. Galardi said.

Adam replied, knowing that would not be a good idea. "Mrs. Galardi, with all due respect, Mr. Galardi doesn't want to bring his department in on this because it's top secret. Only he and Captain Miller are aware of this, and not even Captain Miller knows about the transport machine. If it gets out the transport machine could fall into the wrong hands, and that could endanger the world."

"Does anyone have any suggestions?" Jackie asked.

Josh answered quickly. "We'll have to go after him."

"I agree," Adam said without hesitation.

"Who has to go after him, and how do you wish to accomplish this when Chicago is over one thousand miles away from us?" Billy asked with concern.

"We need a volunteer, and they will have to travel by way of the transporter," Adam said with conviction.

No one said a word. No one looked at each other. No one even seemed to breathe.

"What if the machine doesn't work right and something happens to us?" Billy asked anxiously.

"The machine is in perfect working condition. We must find out what happened to Mr. Galardi. We shouldn't even have waited this long," Adam responded.

There was a slight moment of silence and then...

"I'll go!" Josh volunteered.

"Excellent!" Adam said as he continued. "You must call your..."

Josh cuts Adam off. "I already have permission from my father. I called him an hour ago and informed him that this might happen. I'm ready. Let's not wait any longer."

Everyone just stared at Josh. No one ever thought that Josh was that sort of person. He was so quiet, but it now appeared that he had been thinking a lot about it.

Adam went right to work. "Billy, bring up Mr. Galardi's exact location. Josh, this is for you."

Adam pulled out another watch and earpiece and handed it to Josh. He also gave him a clear packet of liquid gel.

"This watch is similar to Mr. Galardi's watch. It doesn't have all the functions, but it will allow you to communicate with us. We will also be able to see live video action because the satellite will use the watch as a video transmitter. As for this gel pack, just try and smear a small amount somewhere on Mr. Galardi's skin. I'll explain what it does later. You have everything you'll need, and we will have our eye on you at all times."

"I trust you, Adam." Josh said very calmly.

Josh made his way over to the C-1 transport door and waited for it to open.

Adam began pushing buttons and doing his thing. "Kelly, stay close by, and Jackie, move to your sector and prepare to engage power on my mark."

The C-1 transport door opened and Josh stepped inside. No one was worried. There were no second thoughts. The team was in mission mode and ready to accomplish this mission.

Adam nodded at Josh, and Josh nodded back. The C-1 door closed. Adam began the process. "Kelly, key in the target point."

"Completed," Kelly replied.

"Jackie, increase power to Modulation Level 2," Adam ordered.

"Power increased to Level 2," Jackie responded.

"Here we go," Adam continued. "Jackie, get ready to increase power to Level 4 on my mark. Get ready...get ready...not yet...Now! Increase power to Level 4."

"Power increased to Level 4." Jackie reported.

"Transport complete," Adam said, then directed instructions to Billy. "Billy, punch in the video cam and put it on the big screen."

Within seconds the picture came up on the big screen. The team watched the ground ripple, and the C-1 transport door shot out of the ground with sparks flying everywhere. Lighting bolts were flying around the door, and it finally opened. As the smoke cleared, Josh stepped out of the C-1 transport door and gave a thumbs up to the team.

The entire team cheered for Josh and his successfully completed transport.

"Billy, transfer video transmission from Satellite to Satellite Watch Mode." Adam said.

"Transfer complete."

Adam addressed Josh, "Josh, do you read me?"

"Loud and clear, Adam. This was a piece of cake... and fun, I might add. Where is my subject, AKA, Mr. Galardi?" (AKA stands for "also known as.")

Adam got a picture visual on Mr. Galardi and found him right in front of "Nick Anderson's American Karate Academy." Mr. Galardi was peering in the window.

"Josh, Mr. Galardi should be right behind you— across the street in front of the karate school."

The video cam was on Josh, and the team could see everything that was going on. Josh turned around and spotted Mr. Galardi.

"I see him," Josh replied into his watch.

"We have a visual on him as well," Adam answered. "Go over to him, and we'll follow you on the video cam. We are hearing you great, so don't worry about pointing your watch in any direction; just be natural."

Josh made his way across the street, while the team awaited the contact.

"Why is he just standing there? Wouldn't you think he would do something?" Mrs. Galardi asked.

Adam answered respectfully. "The karate school is our mission. The son is supposed to become a champion karate fighter, and for some reason he is getting mixed up in some bad stuff. Maybe Mr. Galardi is scoping out the place. It seems that Mr. Galardi has found our mission. I'm starting to think we didn't need to send Josh at all."

DJ added, "You're right, he probably was going to scope out the area and then call us."

"I hope he doesn't get mad at us for sending Josh." Dominique added.

Billy announced, "Hold on. Shhh! Josh is about to make contact."

"Mr. Galardi!" Josh called out from only a few steps away.

Mr. Galardi turned around. His face was covered in blood from a cut over his eye.

Shocked, Josh blurted out, "Oh my gosh, what happened to you?"

Mr. Galardi just stared at Josh. "Can I help you with something?"

"I knew it. Something isn't right." Adam remarked to the team.

"It's me, Josh. Are you all right?" Josh questioned him with great concern.

"You must have me confused with someone else." Galardi said.

"You don't know who I am?" Josh asked again.

23

Mr. Galardi paused, not knowing quite how to answer the question. After a brief moment of confusion he responded. "Kid, I'm not sure who I am. I don't know my name. I don't know where I live. I can't remember anything."

The Fighting Chance team was speechless. Mrs. Galardi began to cry.

Josh didn't know what to say, but before he could respond to Mr. Galardi's comment, Nick Anderson, the owner of the karate school, came running out the front door toward Mr. Galardi.

"Sir, are you all right?" Nick asked with concern. "What happened to you? What's your name?"

Mr. Galardi responded the same way as he did to Josh. "I don't know who I am. I don't know what happened. I woke up, and my motorcycle was lying beside me and… and I don't know."

Nick grabbed him by the arm to help him inside. "Come inside so we can get you cleaned up." Nick commented to Josh. "Young man, thanks for your help. Go about your business; we'll take it from here."

Josh just stood there, not knowing what to do, as Nick continued to question Mr. Galardi.

"Sir, do you have a wallet or driver's license or anything?"

Mrs. Galardi responded to what she just heard Nick say. "Oh my gosh! Joseph left his wallet in my car this morning. He has no information on him."

"That could be a good thing, Mrs. Galardi. This way his cover won't be blown. Don't worry, we can take care of everything from back here," Adam commented.

Chapter Four

New Challenges and New Strategies for the Team

Two days later, the entire Fighting Chance team was back at the Zone, including Josh. Mr. Galardi had not regained his memory. Nick Anderson, the owner of the karate school, had taken Mr. Galardi to the doctor. He also hired him as a temporary employee at the karate school to do odds and ends, but mainly to help with the kids and the various training.

Mr. Galardi was not getting paid, but he got to stay in a room in the back of the karate school, and meals were provided for him.

The Fighting Chance team was aware of all this because of the gel pack that Josh had brought with him. Before Josh returned to the Zone, he placed a nonwashable smudge of gel onto Mr. Galardi's skin. This gel had transmitter particles mixed within its substance. This substance, once programmed, allowed Adam and the team to pick up audio dialogue from Mr. Galardi. Because of this they were always aware of his actions.

The Strategy Meeting Begins

The entire team, along with Mrs. Galardi, was discussing the next move of action.

Adam initiated the conversation, "Mrs. Galardi, we must set up camp in Chicago. This is how I see it. Mrs. Galardi, Dominique and Josh must transport to the Chicago location, get a hotel there and immediately enroll in the karate school as students. Enroll them in as many classes as you can so all three of you can be around Mr. Galardi as much as possible. Don't try to bring his memory back by obvious comments like, 'hey, I'm your daughter,' or stuff like that. Just be around him as much as possible, and his memory will come back on its own. That's what I heard the doctor say when he was in the office."

Adam did not tell them that the doctor also said that Mr. Galardi's memory might never return and that only time would tell.

Adam continued. "How do you feel about what I just said?"

Before Mrs. Galardi could answer, Yuri voiced his concern, "What about school?"

Jackie responded to that. "We only have two days left until summer break. I think Mr. Galardi's life is important enough to miss two days of school, especially since we have no tests left and its just going to be like fun days."

"OK, just thought I'd ask." Yuri replied with a smile.

"Let's do it," Mrs. Galardi said.

Adam gave simple but important instructions to the

threesome. "Josh, your job is to become friends with Jonathan Anderson, Nick Anderson's son, and gather any information that you may need to find out why he is messing around with a street gang. Dominique, your job is to have as much conversation with your father as you possibly can. Mrs. Galardi, you must be at every class that these two attend. Wear outfits that Mr. Galardi likes you to wear and familiar clothes that may jog his memory in any way possible. Any questions or comments?"

"Let's get on with it." Josh responded as did the rest.

Immediately preparation begins. While Adam was putting a small suitcase of gadgets together for them to take, Josh got permission from his family and filled them in on all that had to be done. Mrs. Galardi arranged for her sister to stay with the her younger kids. She told her sister that she was taking Dominique to a singing competition in Chicago.

When all the necessary arrangements had been made and the team was ready to send the threesome off to Chicago. It was not only their first mission, but also one without the guidance of their leader, Mr. Galardi.

Adam gave last minute details to everyone. "Mrs. Galardi, I have called and made arrangements with the Marion Hotel, which is one block from the karate school. You will not need a car, and there are two grocery markets within walking distance of the hotel. I hope you don't mind, but I used Mr. Galardi's credit card from the wallet you brought in yesterday."

"I don't mind, Adam. You've done a wonderful job. All of you have done a wonderful job. Mr. Galardi would be and will be proud of you."

"If the three of you will step into the C-1 transport door, you will be in Chicago in less than sixty seconds," Adam said. He continued, "Here you go, Mrs. Galardi. You will need your husband's wallet for identification."

The three entered the C-1 transport door, and the transport process began. Kelly pinpointed the mark, and Jackie engaged power to Level 6.3.

A very successful transport delivered the threesome to the back of the Marion Hotel. They checked into their rooms and, wasting no time, immediately made their way to the karate school.

Chapter Five

The Mission Begins

gain! Again! Again!" Nick Anderson instructed his students with power and authority as they punched and kicked a focus bag, which Mr. Galardi was holding. The focus bag allowed the students to kick a moving object and keep Mr. Galardi from getting hurt.

In walked Josh, Dominique and her mom. They were prepared and ready to enroll in every class possible.

Nick Anderson spotted them, then turned the class over to his oldest son, Mike, who was twenty-four years old, so he could be of assistance to his new customers.

They took a seat and began looking around, trying not to stare at Mr. Galardi. Dominique and her mom did not want to look because they might start crying, so they kept their heads down. Josh on the other hand, changed his mind and made direct eye contact with Mr. Galardi.

Approaching the threesome, Nick Anderson greeted each prospective customer and invited them into his office. When Mrs. Galardi stood to her feet. Mr. Galardi looked her way. He couldn't take his eyes off of her. He was paying so much attention to her that he was not ready for the kick that was headed his way.

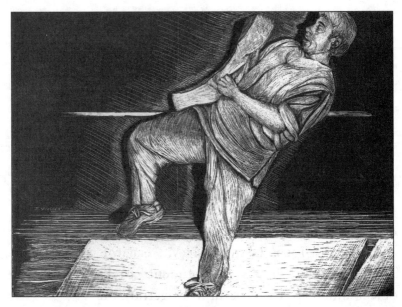

A student kicked the bag and completely knocked Mr. Galardi off balance and onto the floor.

Josh began to chuckle under his breath.

"You gotta pay attention, sir," the student commented, as the rest of the class laughed at the funny mishap.

The next day, the team wasted no time. Mrs. Galardi was watching the class. Dominique had been placed in the group of students who were working on the focus bag, which was being held by her father. He didn't look very good. He was unshaven, and his hair was messy.

There was still no sign of Jonathan.

It was Dominique's turn to kick the bag. She knew a few of the kicks that the rest of the students were doing because her father had taught them to her in the past.

Dominique stepped up to the bag, but first addressed Mr. Galardi. "Excuse me, sir. What is your name?"

Mr. Galardi hesitated for a moment. "They call me Bruce... Bruce Banner.

One of the students spoke up, "He has amnesia, so we call him Bruce Banner. Like the guy who was the Hulk when he wasn't the Hulk? You know... he just wandered around. That's why. Besides, Mr. Anderson named him that."

Dominique began to kick the bag. One of the instructors commented on her kicks. "You kick that bag pretty good for a white belt. Who taught you that kick?"

"My dad," Dominique answered, and she kept kicking.

A young man entered the place and was stopped by Mr. Anderson. They appeared to know each other. Mr. Anderson didn't seem to be very pleased with the young man.

Mr. Anderson grabbed the young man by the shirt and pulled him into his office. That got Josh's attention, as well as Mrs. Galardi's.

Josh moved closer to the door of the office, and he could hear the man yelling at the young man.

That's got to be Jonathan, Josh said to himself.

Josh's concentration was interrupted when the instructor, Mike, called an end to the class.

After the class was released, Dominique made her way over to her mother. Mr. Galardi was right behind her. Mrs. Galardi began to get nervous, but she composed herself very well.

"Your daughter did very well for her first day," Mr. Galardi commented. He extended his hand to Mrs. Galardi. "My name is Bruce. I'm one of the helpers around here."

31

She accepted his handshake while doing her best to stay composed. "I'm Monica, Dominique's and Josh's mother."

That was an awkward moment. For some reason, Mr. Galardi could not take his eyes off of Monica. His stare was broken when instructor Mike addressed the class.

"For anyone who is interested, there will be a stretching class for those who wish to increase their flexibility. I recommend that new students participate. Bruce will be available to help with the stretching if there are not enough partners. Also, don't forget: The National Championships are this weekend. Since my father is always honored at these events, my two brothers, Kevin and Jonathan, along with myself, will be competing. We would appreciate as much support from all of you as possible."

Dominique turned to Mr. Galardi. "If I take the class, will you be my stretching partner?"

Mr. Galardi looked at Monica. "Sure, if it's all right with your mom."

Monica gave the OK, and Dominique and her dad walked toward the stretching class.

Jonathan came out of his father's office dressed in his karate uniform with his black belt around his waist. He didn't look very happy, and he called out to the class, "Does anyone need a stretching partner?"

"I do," Josh said, before anyone else could speak out.

"C'mon, let's go," Jonathan instructed, not very happy from the conversation he had just had with his father.

Dominique was on the floor, doing some simple stretches. The warm-ups allowed for some conversation.

"Are you a black belt too, Bruce?" Dominique asked.

"I don't think so. However, I feel like I might be able to do some of these kicks and punches that the rest of the students are doing."

"Have you tried?"

"No, I haven't, although I've thought about it." Bruce, AKA Mr. Galardi, responded as he continued. "What's your dad like?"

"He's confused right now," Dominique added. "He and my mom are not together."

"Oh, I see. I'm sorry to hear that."

"No, you're not," Dominique responded, catching Mr. Galardi off guard. "You like my mom. I can tell."

"No, I don't...I mean, she's very pretty, but I don't like her. I don't even know her."

"Let me rephrase the question. You'd like to get to know her, wouldn't you?"

Mr. Galardi didn't answer the question. He just kept stretching.

"Can I suggest something to you?" Dominique asked, then continued without waiting for an answer. "Do you own a razor and a comb and stuff like that?"

"Yes, I do. Why? Would you like to borrow them?"

"No! But if you wish to attract attention from people like my mom, I suggest you use them."

Mr. Galardi smiled at Dominique, but then stopped smiling. "Why are you so interested in me meeting your mom?"

Dominique retorted, "Who said I was interested? By the way you were staring at her, I thought you were interested. I thought I would suggest that if you want the attention of a beautiful woman like my mother you might want to consider shaving and combing your hair. You know...the hygiene thing."

"You are a very bright young lady, but right now, the only thing I'm interested in is figuring out who I am. I think that's going to take up enough of my time."

Dominique nodded, and then responded with a helpful suggestion. "I heard somewhere that if you try and concentrate too much, it creates a mental block. Just relax, you'll figure it out."

Chapter
Six

"I'm Never Good Enough.
I'll Show Him!"

It was Saturday afternoon, and there were over five thousand people in attendance, watching and cheering for the competitors at this year's annual National Karate Championship.

Much of the competition had been completed, and it was now down to the final bouts of the day. The center ring was set up for the under-eighteen black belt championship competition. The Master of Ceremonies for the day was about to announce the first bout to take place.

"Ladies and gentlemen, before we announce the center stage action I would like to take this time to introduce to you one of karate's most recognizable sons: the undefeated grand champion for ten years in a row, the one, the only...Mr. Nick Anderson!"

Nick took a bow and the crowd went wild. Flash bulbs were going off and the cheers were almost deafening.

"In the center ring, fighting for this year's National Grand Championship in the black belt under-eighteen division, defending his title from last year...fifteen-year-old Sean Seaver."

Sean's supporters and some of the participating crowd cheered for him.

"His opponent is none other than the son of National Grand Champion, Nick Anderson: fourteen-year-old Jonathan Anderson." The crowd cheered much louder for Jonathan just because he was Nick Anderson's son. Of course, this put more pressure on both Jonathan and his famous father.

As the fight instructions were taking place, Mr. Galardi stayed with Nick Anderson to assist and help him in any way necessary.

Dominique, Josh and Mrs. Galardi, along with others from the karate school, were sitting around the ringside, waiting to support Jonathan's big match.

Dominique looked over and smiled at her dad as she noticed that he had shaved and combed his hair. He was looking more like himself.

Dominique spoke to her mom concerning matters with her dad. "Mom, you gotta at least act like you're interested."

"Honey, the only thing your father is interested in right now is figuring out his name. You said it yourself. Besides, what if he asked me out and ended up not liking me? Then when he snapped out of it, he might not want me anymore."

"You've got to be kidding, right? How many times have we heard him say at home, 'come and give me a kiss, my true love' and all that other sappy stuff he always said to you. If that's true love, he would never be able to see anything but stars in his eyes for you."

The action in the center ring was not going very well for Jonathan. He was down in points, and the round was almost over. It was only a three-round fight, and the winner was determined by points.

The horn to end the second round sounded, and Jonathan returned to his sideline to receive instructions from his father.

"What in the world are you doing out there? You are embarrassing me, son. You're fighting like a white belt. Focus! You get out there and bring in the win! I will accept nothing less," Nick Anderson said angrily and with authority.

The fight continued, and Jonathan's situation had not really changed. The competition was nearing its end, and not only did Jonathan not catch up in points, but he also had also fallen farther behind.

The horn sounded, signaling the end of the round and the match. Jonathan returned to his corner with his head down. He had tears in his eyes.

"I did the best I could; I just couldn't pull it off," Jonathan said, very frustrated.

Mr. Galardi reached out to Jonathan. "Don't be so hard on yourself. You did the best you could. You'll get 'em next time."

Nick Anderson stepped in. He was loud and angry, and he didn't care who heard him. "Your best wasn't good enough. You are an embarrassment to yourself, the school and to me. Both of your brothers won today. They didn't even let their opponents get a single point. Get your stuff and walk home. Think about your actions.

Maybe the walk will knock some sense into you."

Jonathan had to walk to the center of the ring, along with Sean Seaver so that the winner could be announced and made official.

The announcer proclaimed the winner: "The winner of this year's National Karate Championship in the under-eighteen division is Sean Seaver."

The crowd cheered for the great job Sean did in the ring.

As Jonathan left the center ring, Josh heard Adam speaking to him in his earpiece. "Josh, do you read me?"

"Loud and clear, Adam."

"I don't like the activity outside the south entrance of the building you are in. There is a group of young people hanging around. They have been waiting for a while, and

I am picking up knives on them. I wasn't concerned at first because I thought they were competition knives, but now I am positive they are illegal weapons."

"Should I be concerned?" Josh answered.

Adam responded to Josh, not really answering his question. "Jonathan is heading toward that door. I have a feeling they are waiting for him. Go with him, and tell Dominique to stay with her mom."

"Will I be safe?" Josh asked with concern.

"Need you even ask?" Adam said as he continued. "You will know of any danger happening around you before you even ask.

Adam turned to Billy. "Enter System Code 3 now." Billy entered the code as Adam continued with Josh. "Josh, there is a small red button on the bottom of your watch. Push and hold it in for three seconds."

Josh pushed the button as Adam requested. "What did I just do?" Josh inquired.

"It's a neurological magnetic wave sensor that you just activated. I will be able to pick up the behavior of those around you and detect any violent actions that may take place. It gives me time to act and not have to wait for the last minute."

Josh filled in Dominique and Monica, and then headed out with Jonathan.

Adam was right; there were four friends waiting for Jonathan right outside the door.

Josh ran up behind Jonathan. "Hey, Jonathan, do you mind if I hang with you?"

Jonathan looked at Josh, and before he could answer,

one of the other guys answered first. His name was Stitch, and he was about eighteen years old. "You can hang with us. We can use another body. Is that cool with you, Jonathan?"

"Yeah, just don't repeat what you hear or see. Got it?"

"No problem," Josh said quietly.

Back inside, Nick Anderson signed the last few autographs. Mr. Galardi was standing right beside him in case he needed anything.

As Mr. Anderson finished the last autograph, he turned to Mr. Galardi. "Listen, Bruce. I understand your concern for my son, but this is a family matter, and it really isn't any concern of yours. Do you understand what I am saying?"

"Yes, sir, I apologize. I just figured—" Mr. Galardi was cut off by Mr. Anderson.

"Again, this is a family matter. Don't figure."

"Yes, sir," Mr. Galardi respectfully responded, then continued. "I'm going to walk home this evening, if that's OK with you, Mr. Anderson."

"That's fine," Mr. Anderson answered, totally focused on the recent embarrassing upset.

"Hey, Bruce!" Dominique yelled from a short distance.

Mrs. Galardi reacted when she heard Dominique's voice call out. "What are you doing?" Monica asked, as Mr. Galardi made his way over to the twosome.

Dominique answered with confidence. "I don't want to walk home alone. Why should we have to take a cab when I have my big strong, police officer Daddy with us who can walk us and doesn't even know who he is?"

Dominique thought for a moment, then realized what

she was saying; She changed her mind. "You're right. We'll take a cab."

As she hailed a cab, her father tapped her on the shoulder. "Is everything all right?" He added, "You yelled out like you saw a dead rat or something like that."

As soon as Mr. Galardi said "dead rat," he had a flashback of the old mill when Dominique screamed at the dead rat on the floor. He quickly snapped out of it. It wasn't enough to jar his memory.

"Are you all right?" Dominique asked with concern.

"Yes, I'm fine. What did you need?"

"My mom and I were wondering if you could walk us to our hotel. It's just down the street. It's the Marion Hotel."

"Sure, but why are you staying at a hotel?" Mr. Galardi asked.

"It's a long story. So how about it, can ya?" Dominique asked, all cutesy with her own plan in mind.

"Well, of course I will," Mr. Galardi answered.

"It was her idea. I said we could just take a cab." Monica said, embarrassed, even though she was speaking to her own husband.

"Don't be silly. Have no fear, Bruce is here," he answered with a silly gesture.

"Oh brother, what a dork," Dominique said quietly to herself.

"What did you say?" her mother asked sternly.

"I said, 'My brother! My brother.' I was wondering where my brother was, then I remembered he was walking with some friends. Yeah, that's right."

Back at the mill, Adam and the team were picking up some activity that concerned them..

"Adam, I don't like what I'm seeing. There are four people approaching Josh and his friends," Billy said.

"I see, and I wouldn't call them his friends," Adam responded.

"Josh, you are about to encounter some people as soon as you turn the corner. Switch us over to full video cam," Adam alerted.

"Roger," Josh responded.

One of the guys Josh was walking with turned and reacted to Josh's comment. "What did you just say?"

Josh had to think fast. "I said 'Roger.' I thought that was your name. Anyway, I think we are about to meet some people right around this corner."

"How do you know?" Stitch asked.

"I don't know. Just an instinct." Josh replied.

As they turned the corner, four boys confronted them. Stitch spoke first, "We weren't supposed to meet here."

The four boys were some of the leaders of Stitch's gang, and they brought a seventeen-year-old kid who was going to fight Jonathan. If Jonathan didn't back down and could last fifteen minutes with this kid, they would let Jonathan in the gang.

Stitch got things moving. "Are you ready?" he asked Jonathan.

"Yeah!" Jonathan responded, "Give me a minute."

Jonathan turned around to gather his thoughts, and Josh approached him.

"What are you doing, man? You don't want to get

42

involved with these people," Josh said, trying to change his mind.

"Stay out of it. You heard my father. You actually think I care what he or anyone thinks? I'm never good enough for him or my brothers. Today I do my own thing. I make a name for myself."

"Make a name..." Trying to make him understand, Josh was cut off as Jonathan walked away. Jonathan's anger and pride had overtaken his common sense. Just before Jonathan reached the boys, he turned to Josh and said, "Watch this."

His anger was steaming. All he could think of was what his father had said to him. Jonathan looked at Stitch. "Let's do it."

A seventeen-year-old boy named Double K was not only bigger than Jonathan, but also had no fear. He was even rather cocky.

"C'mon, punk. Let's see what you've got," Double K said as he moved into position.

Jonathan didn't even wait a moment. He attacked Double K with a blur of punches and kicks. He round-kicked Double K in the stomach, causing him to bend over. Then Jonathan upper-cut Double K in the chin and continued punching until Double K fell to the ground, semi-conscious. Jonathan did not continue going after him. He waited to see if Double K was going to get up or not.

It was obvious that K was on the ground to stay. Stitch and the rest of the guys just stood there, amazed at what just happened.

"Dude, you dropped Double K in less than one

minute. No one has ever done that!" one of the guys said.

A few of the guys got Double K to his feet. Double K just nodded to Jonathan in respect to the fight.

Everyone gathered around Jonathan, praising him and welcoming him to the so-called street family.

Jonathan smiled and quickly returned to the cheers of the street—cheers he wished he would have gotten in the center ring,. especially from his father.

Stitch shook hands with Jonathan and gave him a "your with us," kind of hug. "I'll catch you tomorrow, bro," Stitch said as they walked away.

They left, and Jonathan turned to look at Josh, standing with his hands in his pockets. Jonathan knew he was wrong, and he knew that Josh was not happy with him. Jonathan's moment of glory was over and his pride was satisfied for now. That would drag him closer and closer to a point of no return...a point of total destruction.

Jonathan had a million thoughts going through his head. As he turned around and started walking, he called out to Josh, "Are you coming or not?"

Josh reluctantly went along with him.

Chapter Seven

After Much Confusion, the Fog Is Lifted

Dominique and her mom and dad arrived at the hotel. "I'm going to run upstairs and shower real quick, OK? See ya, Mom. See ya, Daaa—Bruce." Dominique ran off, biting down on her teeth as she realized she had almost blown it.

"Thanks, Bruce, for walking us home," Monica said, feeling a little awkward for calling him Bruce.

"My pleasure," Mr. Galardi said, as he put his hand out to shake hers.

They shook hands, and he froze for a moment. Another flashback occurred. He couldn't make it out, so he shook it off.

"Are you all right?" Monica asked, knowing what was going on.

Monica held on to his hand for a moment. She was madly in love with her husband, and she only wished he knew who she was. Without thinking she continued. "Would you like to join me for a cup of coffee? My treat."

She waited, hoping he would respond with a positive answer.

Mr. Galardi didn't really know what to say. He opened

his mouth and tried to speak, "I'd . . . I'd love to. Yes, thank you."

It seemed like forever, but when he answered, she gave a sigh of relief.

There was a balcony right above them, and Dominique was watching the whole thing take place. "Yes!" she responded. She liked what she heard, then ran off to her hotel room.

Two hours passed, and Monica and Bruce were still drinking coffee and talking with each other. Josh had long since come back to the hotel and was in the room playing video games with Dominique.

Back at the table, the conversation continued. "So you won't tell me what happened to your husband. That's OK." He paused.

Monica had both her hands around her coffee cup. Mr. Galardi didn't say a word. He placed his hands around her hands and held on to them as he continued to look at her. She felt very familiar with this. It was the same love and affection he had given her for the past nineteen years.

"You are very beautiful and warm and compassionate. May I ask you a question?" said Mr. Galardi.

"Yes," Monica answered, not knowing what to expect.

"May I kiss you, please?"

"Yes," she responded, holding back the tears in her eyes.

The table was very small, and he leaned over just a bit and gave her a soft warm kiss on the lips. He pulled away and just looked at her. He was very confused as to why he just did that with a woman he had just met a few hours ago.

"I . . . I don't know why I just did that. Do I know you? Have we met before? I feel very comfortable around you."

Monica didn't know how to answer the question. "I'd better be going," she said. "I enjoyed talking with you, I'll see you tomorrow."

"Why?" Mr. Galardi asked, still very confused.

"Karate class," she replied with a smile.

"Oh, yeah," he answered.

As she walked away Mr. Galardi couldn't take his eyes off her. One, because she was so beautiful, and two, because he couldn't figure out if he knew her or not.

It was 6 P.M. the next day, and all the students, ranging from children to adults, were warming up for their class.

Nick Anderson walked to the front of the room to address the class. "I am going to have to be excused from teaching this evening. I have a very important meeting, but I leave you in good hands with our new heavyweight National Grand Champion: my son, Mike Anderson. He will be joined by the new middleweight champion: his younger brother, my other son, Kevin Anderson." The class cheered for both of them. "Jonathan, help your brothers out with whatever they need."

Once again Jonathan felt like a loser and had to swallow his pride in front of the students.

Nick Anderson smiled at the class and exited the building.

As the class progressed, the students were taking turns kicking and punching the focus bag that Kevin Anderson was holding. Bruce was over in the corner of the room, tightening the screws on the banister rail that the students used to stretch their legs.

Dominique was kicking the bag, and Kevin responded, "Your kicks are pretty good, young lady. Keep up the good work."

"Thank you," she responded. Then she continued with a question that no one expected her to ask. "Mr. Anderson, I would like to see Bruce kick the bag. He never does anything but help out. Would that be possible?"

Bruce turned around as he heard his name mentioned. Kevin and Mike were in a good mood, still riding on the wave of their championship wins.

"I don't see why not," Mike said, responding to Dominique's question. "Who would like to see Bruce give this bag a try?"

The entire class responded with a positive, "Yes!"

"C'mon up here, Mr. Bruce. Let's see what you can do!" Kevin said..

Dominique took a seat right in the front row next to Josh. Josh looked at her, wondering what was going to happen.

Mike showed Bruce how to throw the round kick. He demonstrated it by kicking the bag Kevin was holding.

"You see how that works? It's simple. Just pivot on your back foot and put your hip into it. Go ahead. Give a good hard kick."

Bruce was a little reluctant to throw the kick. He took a deep breath and let loose. The kick had so much power that it threw Kevin clear off his feet, and he landed flat on his back.

Both Mike and Kevin stood in shock, while Bruce couldn't figure out where that came from. The rest of the class started to clap and cheer.

Dominique looked over at Josh. "That's my dad," she said proudly.

Mike helped his brother to his feet.

"Kevin, are you all right?" Bruce asked, feeling bad for what just happened.

"I'm fine. That was an awesome kick, Bruce," Kevin said. He added. "I want you to try that again. Let me take a better stance. I wasn't expecting that." Kevin motioned to his brother, Mike. "Stand behind me and support my back on this next kick. OK, Bruce, let's see that again."

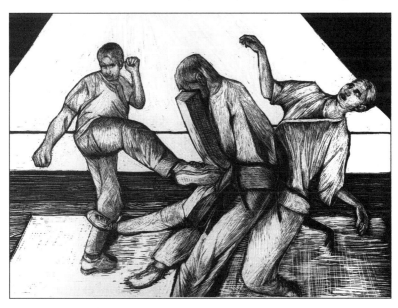

Bruce took his stance and unloaded another kick, sending both brothers to the floor. The class cheered again, and both brothers got up again, this time having had enough.

"Who in the world is this guy?" Mike asked the class jokingly, but was actually serious. "No longer should we call him Bruce Banner, the wanderer called the Hulk. Now he's Bruce Lee, the man who kicks like an explosive cannon."

Bruce smiled as the class cheered him on. He humbly went back to the banister that he was tightening and finished his job.

After class the people mingled and conversed with each other as always. Mr. Galardi put the screwdriver into his pocket and made his way over to Monica so that he could speak with her before she left for the evening.

Josh went over to Jonathan, who was on his way to the locker room to get changed.

"Jonathan!" Josh called out as he made his way over to him. "You want to hang out and do some video games? You gotta give me a chance to at least try and beat you."

"Not tonight, man. Gotta meet some friends," Jonathan said.

"Friends or enemies?" Josh fired back.

Jonathan didn't know what to say. "I just gotta do what I gotta do, all right?"

"Whatever," Josh answered, knowing he couldn't force Jonathan to do something he didn't want to do.

Bruce was in the middle of a casual conversation with Monica while two young girls were having a conversation next to them. Bruce brought his casual conversation to a more serious question. "Monica, would you be interested in having coffee with me again?"

She smiled. "Let's do better than that. Why don't you join me for dinner tonight? Dominique has a friend who is coming over to hang out and watch TV, and I will be dining alone. The hotel owes us a complimentary dinner anyway, because they didn't have a non-smoking room available for us when we checked in."

"I would love to have dinner with you. Please allow me to finish cleaning up this place and get cleaned up, and I'll be right over," Bruce said with anticipation

The two girls next to Monica were having their own conversation, and one of them said to the other, "What are your sisters' names?"

Bruce was still smiling at Monica, and before the girls could answer, Bruce instantly lost his smile and answered their question for himself.

"Nicole and Jenna," he said, not even knowing why he said that. He looked up at Monica. "Why did I just say that? Who are Nicole and Jenna?" Bruce asked with great confusion, not remembering that those were the names of his two other daughters.

Monica could tell that he was getting very frustrated with himself. "Don't stress yourself out. It will come to you. Just relax."

Mr. Galardi smiled at her. "You're right. OK then, I'll see you in about an hour."

Everyone had left, and Mr. Galardi was making his way to the locker room to shut off the lights and make sure the back door was locked. When he went to check the back door, he found it unlocked. Confused as to why, he opened the door and stepped outside to check things out.

"Bruce, it's cool. I'll be there in just a minute. Don't lock me out."

It was getting dark, and Bruce couldn't see who was talking to him. "Who is it?" he shouted back.

"It's me, Jonathan. I'll be right there," he said to Bruce, and then he continued to speak to his friends. "I gotta go. I'll catch you guys tomorrow. I'm in, don't worry."

Jonathan made his way toward the building and entered through the back door, only to find Bruce sitting on a chair next to the lockers.

"Mind if I talk to you for a second?" Bruce politely asked Jonathan.

"No, what's up? Gotta make it fast. My brothers are going to be here to pick me up soon."

"Tell me what's going on." Bruce said to him.

"Nothing." Jonathan answered. "Can't a guy hang out with a few friends?"

"I'm not the kind of guy who makes people do what I think is right. I just say my peace, and you do what you want. At least I think that's what kind of a guy I am."

Jonathan and Bruce both laughed because Jonathan was getting advice from a guy who couldn't even remember his own name.

"That's cool, Bruce, bring me what you got." Jonathan said..

"This is what I think," Bruce continued. "I don't think you even want to hang out with guys like that. I think you just want to be accepted by your father like he accepts and respects your older brothers. Now, don't interrupt. I think I'm on a roll."

Jonathan chuckled again as Bruce continued.

"I know it hurt you the other day when you lost your match and your father embarrassed you in front of all those people. You were angry, and you felt like you didn't fit in anywhere. You felt like you were a loser, and being the competitive person that you are, you went all out to prove that you were important and that you would get respect from someone somewhere, no matter what it took. How am I doing so far?" Bruce said with a smile.

"Not too bad," Jonathan said, pausing for a moment as he tried to shift the blame so that he didn't have to accept responsibility for his actions. "You don't know my father. He is the best in the world at what he does, and he expects us to be the best with him. My father doesn't accept my abilities where they are right now. It's always something negative when he speaks to me. I'm never good enough. I'm never as good as Mike or Kevin. They were better than me when they were my age. I can't take this anymore. I'm not sure this is even what I want to do. At least my friends think I'm somebody. I don't know. They—"

Bruce interjected. "They feed your pride, and they tell you what you want to hear. They don't care about you. You just make them look better, and they like you around for that. I understand how you feel. What you need to understand is: That's false joy. Do you know what I'm saying? It leads to a bad ending."

Jonathan continued, expressing his feelings. "I gotta be the best at something. It may as well be this."

Bruce chose his words carefully. "Let me just say this. You are fourteen years old. You can grow and become a great champion someday, but you will never know if you give up or if you're dead. And if for some reason you never become number one, which I know you will, then being number two at something that can lead to something great, with the hopes of being number one, is better than being number one at something that will lead to a destructive ending. Your father loves you, and he feels this sort of discipline is what you need in order to become who you are destined to be. Who am I to say if he is right or wrong? But I can say this, and whether you receive this or not is up to you: Jonathan, your success in life does not depend on what others think of you, not even your father; your success in life depends on what you think of you. If others give up on you, that's OK. If you give up on you, it's over. Your father is a good karate man. He's not the best. There is always someone out there better, he just hasn't met them yet. If he ever meets them, he will accept it for the time being, and then he will try harder to better himself. That's how we grow. We must strive to better ourselves in things that make us a better person and this world a better place, not the things that give us momentary fame that lead to a bad ending. No short cuts. No quitting. I'm not telling you what to do, I just hope you'll come to the understanding of what you need to do."

"That makes a lot of sense, Bruce. Who are you, anyway?"

"I wish I knew. The question is . . . who are you?" Bruce answered as he got up to walk out. "Gotta go, kid. Got a

54

hot date."

Jonathan smiled and shook his head at the way Bruce could be so serious and then come off joking out of nowhere.

Mr. Galardi ran up the street to make up the time he lost talking with Jonathan. On his approach to the Marion Hotel, not a five star hotel but still a high quality establishment, he stopped running and began a fast-paced walk, which segued into a comfortable casual strut.

There were several bell captains standing outside the hotel, welcoming the guests and making arrangements for their luggage to be placed in their rooms.

Mr. Galardi approached the front door with excitement, anticipating a nice evening with Monica. Just before he grabbed hold of the door handle, one of the bell captains who was helping a hotel guest out of his car, offered his services for luggage transportation.

"Would you like me to bring your luggage up to your room, Mr. Gunner?"

Mr. Galardi came to a complete halt. Flashbacks were going back and forth in his mind. He saw pictures of himself as Mr. Gunner in the nerd outfit hanging from the scoreboard grate at the same time he saw Miss Ward yelling at him. He saw himself tripping over a newspaper on the sidewalk and smashing into a tiny little car. It seemed as if he were remembering, but just when he tried to grasp hold of what was happening, everything went blank.

He looked around as if something might help him remember. After a while he got frustrated, then just shook it off and went into the hotel.

Mr. Galardi looked up and saw Monica standing at the front desk, waiting for him. He couldn't take his eyes off of her. She was dressed somewhat casually, and her hair was perfect. *Wow, she is stunning,* Mr. Galardi said to himself.

He approached her, not being able to control what he was about to say.

"Hi, Bruce," Monica said as she turned around and saw him.

"Hi," Mr. Galardi said, staring at her.

She felt a little uncomfortable looking at him while he was staring at her, so she began to speak in order to break the silence.

"Are you ready to sit down?"

Mr. Galardi didn't answer the question. "You look absolutely beautiful."

Her eyes teared up, and she gently lifted her hand to wipe the tears away, but before she could, Mr. Galardi grabbed a napkin from the hostess stand and wiped the tears from her cheek.

They sat and ate. An hour went by, and they were both finished with their meals, including dessert. Monica was drinking coffee, and Mr. Galardi was doing all the talking. "...and then it stopped. I couldn't remember anymore. This has been happening all day. I'm sorry to keep talking about this, but it helps me to destress, I guess."

"I understand. You just talk about it all you want. I'm here for you."

Mr. Galardi didn't respond to her last comment. He

slowly put his head down and rubbed his face with his hands. He took a deep breath and just looked at Monica. He stared at her, and she smiled back because he had been staring at her and telling her how beautiful she was all night.

"Can I say something to you?" Mr. Galardi asked as he shook his head. "As I look at you and realize that no matter how many times I look at you, I am overtaken by your beauty—not only your outer beauty, but your compassion and how sensitive you are."

Tears begin to come from Monica's eyes. She couldn't hold them back any longer.

"I'm sorry for getting all emotional on you, but my husband used to say those things to me."

"Do you miss hearing them from him?" Mr. Galardi said with compassion.

"Very much," she responded, wiping her tears.

"Don't cry anymore, Monica. I'll never leave you, and I'll never stop feeling this way about you. Let me tell you what amazes me. After all these years, I am still madly in love with you."

"Please don't say those things right now," Monica politely asked.

Mr. Galardi looked right into her eyes. "Listen to me," he said with sincere passion. "You're not hearing me. I am madly in love with you, Monica Galardi. I love you, and I love Dominique. I love Nicole, and I love Jenna. I am in Chicago, I live in Florida. The Fighting Chance team is back at the mill, and Jonathan is our mission. Oh my gosh. It's back. I remember everything!"

Monica began to cry, and she couldn't help herself. She got up and went to the side of the table her husband was on and threw her arms around him. "Thank God. Thank God!"

Chapter Eight

He's Back!

Mr. Galardi and his wife were walking out of the elevator holding hands. Monica's head was resting on his arm as they both make their way toward the hotel door.

Dominique really didn't have a friend over to play video games; it was just Josh.

Monica put the key in the door and opened it, calling to the kids. "Kids, I'm back, and Bruce is with me."

"Hey, Bruce, do you want to take me on? Check this game out," Josh asked as he paused the game and looked up at Bruce.

"Feel free to take my place," Dominique said. "I can't beat this guy."

Mr. Galardi made his way to the game, and on the way he tripped over a shoe and knocked a bottle of water off the table. He bent over to pick up the bottle. When he stood up, he got the bottle tangled up in the video wire and yanked it out of the TV. With that, he lost his balance and toppled to the floor, grabbing the bed covering and pulling it off the bed, covering himself completely.

Monica had her hand over her mouth, trying to hide her

laughter, while Josh and Dominique ran over to help him.

"Bruce, are you all right?" Dominique questioned, as she and Josh pulled the bed covering off him.

They cleared his face from the bedding, only to hear him answer in his famous nerdy voice, which for both of them was so familiar. "OK, that didn't work very well for Mr. Gunner, did it?"

Immediately, Josh and Dominique stared at him, knowing, that there was no way Bruce could know that voice or that name.

Dominique threw herself on him, hugging and kissing him. She was so excited that she was screaming, laughing and crying all at the same time.

"What happened? When did it happen?" Dominique asked.

"During dinner," her mom remarked.

"What do we do now?" Josh expressed with more excitement coming from him than ever before.

"We focus, and we continue as planned until the job is done.

I remember everything that happened except when I came out of the C-1 transport door. My motorcycle began to slip on the wet grass, and that's the last thing I remember. I remember Josh standing next to me at the karate school, and Nick coming out to help. I remember everything that happened after that as well."

Mr. Galardi looked over at Josh. "You came after me. I can't believe that. How did you all get here?"

"The transport machine," Dominique answered. "It was awesome. One minute you're there, and the next minute you're here."

"It's nine thirty at night. Do you think anyone is at the Zone?" Mr. Galardi asked, getting right down to business.

"Joseph," Monica answered, "Those kids have not left the Zone since last Saturday when you were transported here. There are two people on watch at all times, and Adam has not left at all. He hasn't even seen daylight."

Joseph Galardi was speechless. The care and concern the Fighting Chance team had given him had moved his heart.

"I could not have asked for a better team than all of you," Mr. Galardi paused, "Wait a minute, can they hear us back at the lab?"

"No." Monica answered. "I have all communications turned off."

"Good thinking," Mr. Galardi said as he continued.

61

"Will the entire team be there tomorrow?"

"Everyone except Dominique and myself," Josh answered.

"Then we will wait until tomorrow to contact them and give them the good news. By the way, does my precinct have any knowledge as to what is going on?"

"Other than the fact that you are on assignment in Chicago, no. Adam made us aware that no one knew of this except Captain Miller, and that if the transport machine fell into the hands of the wrong people, the world would be in great danger. That part I didn't understand fully," Monica commented.

"If the wrong hands get hold of this machine they could deliver very dangerous packages in very important places and not be detected at all," Mr. Galardi responded to his wife's question.

Joseph Galardi grabbed all three of them and put his arms around them, displaying a smile from ear to ear. "I am so glad to be back. You have no idea."

The Next Day

Joseph spent the night at the hotel with his family. The sun was beaming through the hotel window, and Josh was sitting at the small table with his laptop opened and a few of the gadgets Adam sent with him, preparing to begin both audio and visual communication with Adam and the rest of the team.

"Mr. Galardi, the system is set up, and we are ready to make contact with Adam and the rest of the team. Shall I begin the communication process with them?" Josh asked.

"Yes, and let me know when you have the team together. I would like to speak with them. However, don't alert them to me being here," Mr. Galardi commented.

"Yes, sir, Mr. Galardi." Josh responded with a smile, happy that his commander was back in action.

Josh was excited and couldn't wait to see the faces of the team when they heard that Mr. Galardi was back to normal.

Back at the Zone, Jackie was throwing a tennis ball at the wall, trying to amuse herself, while the rest of the team was doing odds and ends in preparation for another day.

A blue light accompanied by a beeping sound went off, and the team moved into position. They gathered around the big screen that was above the C-1 transport door. Billy manned the laptop, and Adam stood to his feet as Kelly joined him with her portable waist computer, ready for orders.

"Go ahead, Josh, we have your signal," Adam said, reacting to the blue light and the beeping sound.

Billy connected Josh to the big screen, and the team could see and hear Josh loud and clear.

"Good morning, everyone. It's a beautiful day in Chicago," Josh commented.

"What in the world is he so happy about this morning?" Jackie asked in a sarcastic tone of voice.

"Well for one, he probably got to sleep in a nice soft bed instead of a sleeping bag on the floor like I did last night." DJ responded in his light-humored way.

"What's on your agenda for this morning?" Adam questioned, wanting to know how to begin planning the day.

Without hesitation, Mr. Galardi stepped in front of the screen and began to speak. "Good morning, team. Adam, I need information on two street thugs: One is named Stitch, and the other is named Double K. Find out who they are and what their real names are. Get backgrounds on both of them, and then link it to who they are running with on the street. Can you pull that together for me as soon as possible?" Mr. Galardi asked as he turned to Dominique and Josh, winked at them and smiled.

Adam, Billy and the rest of the team were staring at the screen, not saying a word. After about twenty seconds, Adam answered with a huge smile and a professional "back in business" kind of attitude, "Yes, sir!"

The team began to cheer and scream. There were smiles on everyone's face.

"Why didn't you call us last night? We all spent the night here, and none of us could sleep because Yuri snored so loudly," Billy said excitedly.

"Sorry, we had our own 'Mr. Galardi is back party,'" Josh said in his dry sense of humor.

"OK, we have to get back to work. The party is over, and we will celebrate when we all get back to Florida," Mr. Galardi said as he continued. "I have to get back to the karate school because Nick is training with Jonathan... some punishment episode or whatever. Anyway, I have to be there to help. Adam, what do you have for us that I need to know?"

"First of all, Mr. Galardi, I think we need to satellite everyone. Josh, there is a plastic case in the bag I sent with you? Do you see it?" Adam inquired.

"Got it right here, Adam," Josh confirmed.

Adam continued with his mind fully engaged on the mission they set out to accomplish several days ago. "Have everyone place one of those paper thin plastic disks on the inside of their left ankle. Once it adheres to your skin it can not be removed without the solution, which is clearly marked in the small bottle that is in the black bag. Josh, make sure all of you have the credit-card-looking device to carry with you at all times. Without that, you will have no privacy. Now, to briefly explain it all to you. The plastic disk allows our satellite camera to pick up audio and visual on you at all times, no matter where you are—inside or out. We can see you clearly up to two hundred meters under the earth's surface. This can happen thanks to the invention of the laser. Of course I upped its ability to go above and beyond what it was intended to do. Now, the credit card device, when activated, by the push of the small button on the lower right side of the card, will stop transmission of the signal, then we will have no contact with you at all. If it is off for a long period of time, it will vibrate, making you aware that we do not have contact with you. If we get no reaction after the vibration, then a beeping signal will go off. Note that there is no way to turn it back on once you engage it to Privacy Mode."

"You never cease to amaze me, Adam," Mr. Galardi said with great astonishment.

"Thank you, Mr. Galardi, but there is more. You must all place the pea-sized transmitter into your ear so that we can communicate verbally with each other."

"Gee, Adam, is that all you got for us?" Dominique asked in a humorous, sarcastic tone.

"For now, I guess," Adam replied, going along with the joke.

Chapter
Nine

Mr. Galardi Is Ready
to Begin the Mission

It was 11:30 A.M., and Nick Anderson was working his son pretty hard. Jonathan was sweating and out of breath at the same time.

"How much longer do we have to go, Dad?" Jonathan asked, breathing heavily with his hands placed on his knees.

"Until you get it right. Bruce, hold the bag, let's do it again."

Jonathan reluctantly moved up to the bag and began punching it again. His punches didn't cause Mr. Galardi to move at all.

Nick just shook his head and stopped the action.

"Stop, Jonathan. Watch...Put your shoulder into it, and don't hold back on the punch."

Nick demonstrated what he was talking about. "Hold the bag tight, Bruce. I'm going to hit it hard," Nick expressed to Bruce.

Nick began to hit the bag with great power, but it still didn't move the bag or Bruce very much.

"You see what I'm talking about, son? Now you try it."

Nick instructed with great authority.

Jonathan really tried, but still his father was not happy.

"No! No! No! Not good enough," Nick reacted angrily.

Jonathan was so frustrated that he was about to cry.

Mr. Galardi, back in full awareness of who he was, politely posed a question to the angry Nick Anderson. "May I make a suggestion in regards to the punching, sir?"

"Go ahead, Bruce, if you think it will help."

"If you don't mind, sir, could you please hold the bag for me?"

Nick took the bag from Mr. Galardi, AKA Bruce, and grabbed hold of it properly.

Bruce began to instruct Jonathan on a few pointers. "If you want to produce great power, then borrow it from a muscle that is stronger than your arm or shoulder. That would be your legs."

"I want him to punch it, Bruce, not kick it." Nick said, interrupting the instructions.

"Yes, sir, I know," Mr. Galardi answered.

Nick nodded for him to continue.

"When you deliver the punch into the bag, push off from your back leg and lunge your punch toward the bag, instead of just placing it there."

Mr. Galardi demonstrated the movement slowly and then inquired of Nick if he could hit it with full power.

"May I?" Bruce asked.

"Go for it," Nick responded, taking a solid stance as he held the bag.

Bruce began to unload his punches into the bag. He kept lunging forward so hard that Nick could barely keep his balance. Bruce threw one last punch into the bag so hard that it sent Nick off balance and onto the floor.

"See what I'm talking about?" Bruce said to Jonathan.

Jonathan nodded his head as he began to laugh. Nick had made his way back to his feet.

"Way to hold that bag, Dad." Jonathan said in a joking way.

"Let's just see if you were paying attention," Nick said, responding to Jonathan's comment.

Nick didn't even acknowledge that Bruce had done a good job, nor did he give Bruce the bag back. Nick held the bag firmly and instructed his son to begin punching.

"C'mon, hit it again."

Jonathan did as Bruce instructed, and his increase in

power grabbed Nick's attention.

"Better. All right, that's all for now. Take five minutes. Bruce, can I see you in my office?"

Both men walked toward the office, and Jonathan just shook his head.

Bruce is in trouble now, Jonathan said to himself.

The door shut firmly. Nick walked behind his desk and had a seat.

"Have a seat," he motioned to Bruce.

Bruce took his seat and just sat with respect and waited for Nick to ask the first question.

Nick took a small breath and rested his chin on his hand, creating a very serious posture. After a moment he posed a question. "May I ask you a question? Nick asked in a soft voice.

"Yes, sir," Mr. Galardi responded respectfully.

"Who in the world are you?" Nick asked, confused.

Mr. Galardi thought about his answer for a moment and then commented with a lighter answer. "Bruce Lee. I used to be Bruce Banner, but your son now calls me Bruce Lee."

"I can't figure you out, and I realize you can't figure you out either. My son told me that you kicked the bag and threw him and his brother onto the floor. Now you punch the bag today, and I end up on the floor. I hope you figure out who you are because I would like to know. By the way, thanks for the tips you gave my son."

"No problem, sir. May I suggest something? Galardi asked, knowing he had to go easy.

"I suppose," Nick responded.

"Your two sons are very good at what they do, and they seem to have gained your respect. I am almost sure Jonathan will achieve that level in time as well. However, he may shut down and revert to other ways of acceptance if he continues to receive negative, rather than positive, response from you."

"Mr. Lee, do you enjoy staying here?" Nick questioned.

"Of course I do," Mr. Galardi answered, knowing where the conversation was going.

"For twenty-five years I have been raising champions in this sport, and I believe I know what I am doing. I will not have my reputation ruined by my own son. Do I make myself clear on that?"

"Yes, sir," Mr. Galardi responded.

"Then if you wish to continue staying here, I suggest that you keep your comments to yourself and just do as I have asked." Nick raised his eyebrows, expressing a gesture that demanded an answer.

"Very well. I apologize for intruding," Mr. Galardi said, knowing he had to approach them another way.

"Please tell my son that I have some work I have to take care of, and that will be all for today."

Mr. Galardi nodded his head and walked out of the office, only to find Josh talking with Jonathan.

"Hey, your dad says that's all for today. He has some work he has to get done."

"Cool," Jonathan commented.

Mr. Galardi looked at the both of them sitting on the floor, knowing they could both use a little fun.

71

"Do you guys want to go to the mall?" Bruce asked.

Jonathan and Josh looked at each other then back at Bruce. "Sure," they both responded.

"Let me get showered first. It will only take a few minutes," Jonathan said, with a glimmer of excitement in his voice because he had something to do that might be fun.

As soon as Jonathan was out of sight, Adam broke in.

"Mr. Galardi, do you read me?" Adam asked, scaring the daylights out of Mr. Galardi.

The team at the Zone laughed back as they watched Mr. Galardi jump as if a bee landed on his nose.

"Whooo! You scared me half to death. I forgot I had this earpiece in," Mr. Galardi was shocked but reacted comically.

"Sorry." Adam added as he continued. "I have your information on the two people you asked about, Stitch and Double K. By the way I think you knocked Mr. Anderson's ego down a few notches."

"Yeah, well, maybe I was a little too aggressive. OK, give me the stats on the boys," Mr. Galardi requested.

"First of all, they are not as far gone as they may seem. Stitch, age eighteen, whose real name is Anthony Thomas, lost his father two years ago in a car wreck that they were in together. He got his name because—are you ready for this—a piece of metal sliced his arm and his father held it together to keep him from bleeding to death. Apparently, when the paramedics arrived on the scene, the father let go and then he died. The newspapers read, 'Father is the stitch that saves boy's life.' I guess he took on that name in honor of his father. He still hasn't recovered from that shock, and I guess that's the way he takes his aggression out. As for Double K, his real name is Kyle Kendrick, AKA Double K. He has no real record. Actually, neither of them have a serious record. They are all heading down a road that will escalate to a destructive end. It sounds like they all need a crash course in anger management."

"Josh told me that Jonathan and these boys are planning to destroy a bunch of new cars at some dealership lot. They're coming toward me right now. I'll get back to you guys later," Mr. Galardi said, as he picked up a magazine and began to read.

Chapter
Ten

The Mall Experience

Jonathan, Josh, Dominique and Bruce, AKA Mr. Galardi, had just entered the mall and were walking past the food court. Jonathan and Josh were a few steps ahead of the others.

"This is going to be really boring with him here. Maybe we should have left him at the karate school," Jonathan commented.

"Maybe so, but your dad wouldn't let you come if Bruce weren't with us," Josh reminded him.

"Yeah, you're right. Maybe we can ditch him and meet up with them later," Jonathan said, planning his strategy.

"Hey you guys, wait up," Bruce called out to them.

They stopped and turned around, waiting for Bruce to catch up. Jonathan already looked quite annoyed. He hadn't even been there for five minutes, and Bruce was already cramping his style.

"You guys want to do something fun and crazy?" Bruce asked.

"What do you have in mind?" Jonathan questioned.

Bruce, knowing exactly what he was going to do, answered, "You see this shoe store to my left? I just heard the manager talking, and one of their employees did not come in today; they are short handed."

"So what are you going to do?" Jonathan wanted to know.

"Josh, give me your glasses," Bruce said.

Josh handed Bruce his glasses but had to keep it cool and not give away what was about to happen.

Bruce put the glasses on, leaving them half-way down his nose. He then wet his hands in the water fountain and matted his hair so that it looked kind of dorky. After a moment of prepping, Josh and Dominique looked at a Mr. Gunner with hair. They couldn't even slip a little.

"You look like a dork," Dominique said, letting out a little laugh.

"Thank you. That was very kind of you to say," Bruce said in his nerdy Mr. Gunner voice.

"Oh my gosh," Jonathan said with his hand over his mouth. "What's he going to do?"

Bruce answered in his normal voice. "You guys gotta go in the store and act just like you're shopping for shoes. Don't lead on like you know me. Got it?"

They all acknowledged and understood what they had to do.

The threesome entered the store and began looking at the various sneakers that the store sold.

Even though Josh and Dominique had seen him in action before, they always liked a good laugh, and laugh they did as Bruce walked into the store with his glasses halfway down his nose and his hair matted down. He really hadn't done anything funny yet, however, the anticipation of what was about to happen was building.

Bruce was approached by one of the store workers.

"Can I help you find something, sir?"

Thinking quickly, Bruce looked at her name badge: She was also the store manager.

In his nerdy voice he answered very politely. "Ah, yes. I am looking for a store manager by the name of Melissa Waldridge."

"How can I help you? I'm Melissa."

"I am Joseph Gunner, and actually, how can I help you? I was sent over from the west store, reason being they said you were a little short-handed. I am not trained on the register. However, I will be able to bring sales to you and allow someone else to ring them up."

Melissa was somewhat confused as she answered. "I was not aware of anyone coming from the west store. You know what? That's fine. We are so busy, I can use an extra hand. Just work the floor, and we can work out the details later."

Jonathan looked at Josh and couldn't believe that it really worked.

"Oh my gosh, he is actually going to do it!" Jonathan said.

"No way!" Josh remarked with a huge smile on his face.

Bruce made his way over to a mother and her child. "How can I help you, ma'am?" Bruce asked in his nerdy voice.

Before the woman could even answer, Bruce stirred up a conversation with her little girl. "What kind of shoes do you want to see on those precious feet?" Bruce asked the little girl, who was around seven years old.

"I don't know," said the little girl.

"The pair she has on now has holes in the bottom, and she doesn't like anything I show her," the mother said, frustrated with her daughter.

"Well, let's just see what we can do for this young lady. What's your favorite color?" Bruce asked her.

"Purple," the little girl said, with her finger in her mouth.

"You just come right over here and let Joseph find you the perfect pair of shoes for you."

Jonathan was laughing hysterically. "I can't believe he is really doing this," Jonathan said, enjoying every bit of it.

Bruce pointed to a purple and white shoe that was on the shelf just a bit over his head. Actually, that was the only purple shoe in the store. "How about that one up there? It's a size 13—just your size according to your mom," Bruce said to her.

She kind of wrinkled her nose and looked at her mom.

Bruce reached for the shoe in his clumsy way, and knocked several other shoes off the shelf as he tumbled to the floor himself.

Jonathan was on the floor laughing.

"Don't worry, I'm OK," Bruce shared as he got up off the floor with shoes all over him. "They were just a little out of my reach."

The little girl was laughing, as was her mother.

"Now take your shoe off, and let's see if these fit you."

The little girl slipped her shoe off. Bruce picked it up and put it up to his eye, looking through the hole in the bottom.

"Oh, no! This will never do. Every bug in the world can crawl in this hole and live in this shoe."

Bruce threw the shoe behind him, and the girl began to laugh again. Taking the new shoe, he placed it on her right foot and tied it up, nice and snug.

"And there you have it—one purple shoe with no holes. Do you like it?" Bruce added.

The girl nodded her head, chewing on her finger at the same time.

"Well, that's just wonderful." Bruce commented, clapping his hands together and jumping around like a complete dork. He was jumping in circles, and the little girl was laughing harder and harder along with Jonathan, Josh, Dominique and the rest of the store. Even the managers were laughing at the goofy antics of Bruce, AKA Joseph Galardi.

The mother brought the shoebox to the counter as she laughed. "We have been shopping for two weeks, and we couldn't find anything we liked. We'll be back to this store. That salesperson is wonderful with children."

Bruce, acting very nerdy, made his way over to Josh and the others. Every customer saw him coming, and they immediately walked out of the store.

Bruce went to the counter and walked up to Melissa. She still had smile on her face. "That was great—what you did for that little girl."

"Thank you," Bruce said in his normal voice, catching Melissa off guard. He continued. "I really don't work for your company. I just needed to do this for a young man who was with us. We're trying to cheer him up. I hope you understand," Bruce commented to Melissa.

"I thought something didn't seem right." Melissa smiled. "It's quite all right. Hey, you got a sale on top of it all! I wish we had more salespeople like yourself."

Bruce walked out of the store, only to face Jonathan, who was still laughing.

"Dude, I can't believe you actually did that. Oh my gosh, you are so funny," Jonathan said, trying to wind down his laugh.

Bruce grabbed Jonathan by the hand, and they walked into one of the larger department stores. "You must keep a straight face no matter what. Can you do that?" Bruce asked as he made his way toward a very pretty young saleswoman.

"You wait here with Josh and Dominique while I go over and talk to that girl. Whatever you do, when and if she looks over at you, just nod your head like you have a sore tooth. Got it?" Bruce said as he walked up to the young saleswoman.

"Excuse me, ma'am. This is the men's department, isn't it?" Bruce asked.

"Yes, sir, it is. How may I help you?" the salesgirl replied very politely.

She was a very pretty girl who attracted both Josh's and Jonathan's attention.

"Well, this is kind of embarrassing. Do you see that young man over there...the taller one?" Bruce asked, pointing with his head rather than his finger.

"Yes, oh, he's kind of cute," the saleswoman commented.

" I need to know where your boxers are for his size," Bruce asked, embarrassed.

"There's nothing embarrassing about that. Would he like any special color?" the girl added.

"I don't think he cares. See, he pooped in his pants, and he just needs to change them right away," Bruce said.

The girl looked over in Jonathan's direction in disbelief, only to find him nodding his head and looking as if he were in pain.

The girl looked back at Bruce and began to laugh. "I'm sorry, I can't help it. You're serious, aren't you?" she added.

"Yes, we are," Bruce said in a very serious tone.

The young girl grabbed a pair of boxer underwear and rang them up. She placed them in a bag and gave them to Bruce. The whole time she was ringing them up she had a smile on her face and chuckled from time to time.

"Thank you, sir. Come again, please," the girl said, holding back her big laugh.

Bruce headed toward the threesome, and the girl headed to her other friends who were working there to tell them what just happened.

Bruce, Dominique, Josh and Jonathan all walked out of the store, and Jonathan looked back only to see three girls looking at him and giggling at the same time. He thought they thought he was so cute that the girl went and got her friend so they could all come to look at him.

"Look at those girls. They're all goo-goo-eyed over Jonathan. What did you say to them, Bruce?" Dominique asked, curious to find out.

The threesome focused on the answer they were about to hear while Bruce reached into the bag and pulled out the pair of boxer underwear and handed them to Jonathan. "I told them you pooped in your pants, and you needed new underwear right away."

Jonathan's face turned white, while the other two were laughing so hard they could hardly breath.

About an hour went by, and they were having so much fun they were still laughing. Within the last hour Bruce went up to the ice cream store and ordered a meatball sub, along with a pair of shoes. He went into the sunglass store and asked the salesperson where he could find sunglasses in the mall. The funniest one was when he went into the "Optic Lens" eyeglass place and informed one of the optometrist doctors that he was there for his hemorrhoid surgery.

Jonathan had more fun in the last hour than he had had in a long time.

They were walking in pairs of two. Jonathan and Josh were walking together, and Jonathan was telling Josh that he was wrong about the boring part, and that he was having an awesome time.

Dominique and Bruce were a few steps behind. Dominique wanted to put her arm around her dad and walk with him, but she didn't because he was not supposed to be her dad..

"Dad, that was so funny. Do you really think you should have done the thing about the hemorrhoid surgery?" Dominique asked, laughing as she thought about it.

"Listen, sweetie. Sometimes you have to get down on their level in order for you to bring them up to yours, and if talking about hemorrhoids is what it takes to save a kid's life, then so be it,." Bruce said as he winked at his daughter.

Dominique smiled, understanding exactly what her dad meant.

"You know, your sister is very cute. How old is she?" Jonathan asked very respectfully.

"She'll be fourteen this month, but don't get any ideas. Her father, I mean, our father, won't let her date. Besides, I don't think she likes guys that poop in their pants," Josh answered, trying to cover up his almost big mistake.

"Very funny," Jonathan fired back as he biffed Josh on the head. "That's cool. I understand."

They had been having so much fun, they hadn't even made it to the center of the mall.

There were several hundred people standing around an empty stage waiting for something to happen.

"What's that all about?" Jonathan asked curiously, looking for information that might inform him as to what was going on.

Josh saw a sign that explained that the mall was having a talent search. They were looking for the mall's best singer of the day. The first place winner would receive one hundred dollars in cash, and the second place winner would receive a fifty-dollar shopping spree to any store in the mall.

"It's a singing talent contest or something like that. Oh, man, I hope my sister doesn't see that," Josh said.

"Why?" Jonathan questioned.

"Why?" Josh repeated as he continued. "All she does is sing."

"Is she any good?" Jonathan asked.

"Oh look, Bruce. A singing contest. I want to enter.

Please?" Dominique pleaded.

"Well, there you have it. I guess you're gonna get to see," Josh answered as Dominique hurried to the sign-up table.

Jonathan got really quiet, and Bruce noticed. "What's the problem, Jonathan? You look like you really did mess your pants."

Jonathan smiled. "It's nothing. It's just that singing is my favorite thing to do, and my father doesn't really want me to."

"Are you any good?" Josh asked.

"I don't know. I just love to sing," Jonathan answered.

"Then get up there with Dominique and sign up. Now!" Bruce ordered.

Jonathan hesitated, then smiled and headed toward the sign-up table where Dominique was already in line.

When it was their turn to sign up, the lady explained how the contest worked.

"You will have a selection of songs you can pick from, and if you don't know all the words, don't worry; we will put them up on a small television screen—you can read off of that. It's kind of like karaoke, but it isn't...if you know what I mean." The lady continued, "The audience will be judging you on your vocals and your stage presentation. So get out there and give it your best. Any questions?"

Dominique and Josh shook their heads, "No."

The lady added, "There are only twenty entries, and it looks like you guys came to the right table because if you were in that line you wouldn't have gotten in. Young lady, you are number thirteen. And you are number fourteen," she said to Jonathan. "We should be starting in about fifteen minutes or so."

After about forty-five minutes it was Dominique's turn to sing. She had chosen the song, "Somewhere Over the Rainbow." Dominique was not one bit nervous. She loved to sing, and was about to show it.

As she stepped onto the stage the crowd gave her a small cheer. The music started, and Dominique began to sing. Her voice was so incredible that before she got even ten words out the crowd applauded.

Jonathan's eyes were glued to her. He loved anything to do with music, and he was hypnotized by Dominique's voice.

As the song continued toward the ending, Dominique hit a high note, and the crowd went wild—really wild. When the song was finished the crowd couldn't contain themselves. This almost fourteen-year-old girl just brought the house down.

Dominique put the microphone back in its place and exited the stage. She passed Jonathan on her way down.

"No way. That was totally awesome," Jonathan said as he made his way onto the stage.

"Thank you," Dominique said, appreciating the compliment.

Bruce was somewhat nervous for Jonathan. He wondered if the kid had any talent, since he had never heard him sing. Some of the kids who sang before them were not very good, and the crowd let them know it.

Jonathan had chosen the song, "My Girl." With his

mike in his hand, the music started, and Jonathan began to sing.

Much to everyone's surprise, his voice was awesome. The crowd let out a small cheer, announcing the fact that they liked his voice.

As Jonathan continued, he did something different with the song. Right in the middle of the song he began to rap. It caught the crowd off guard. They didn't expect that because that was not how the song went, but it was so good that they began to cheer even louder.

Jonathan went back to singing the melody and hit a few incredible notes. That sent the crowd into a cheering frenzy as his song came to an end.

After another half-hour passed, all the contestants came back to the stage, and the judges picked the top best three.

Jonathan and Dominique were among the three top best.

One of the judges made his way onto the stage to let the audience judge who would get first and second place by the applause level.

The judge puts his hand over the third girl's head, and the crowd let out a nice applause. The judge then put his hand over Jonathan's head; the crowd went crazy. The cheering went on for a while and then finally died down. When the judge put his hand over Dominique's head, the crowd became deafening as well.

The cheers and applause were so close that the judge once again held his hand over Dominique and Jonathan to show the crowd that the race for first was close and that their cheers must make the difference.

The cheers for both singers wear deafening. It was close, but more obvious this time, that Dominique had won first and Jonathan had won second. As the two made their way off the stage, Josh and Bruce were waiting for them.

Before Josh or Bruce could get to them, a woman in a very nice business suit, approached the teens. "Are you two here with a parent or someone over the age of eighteen?" the lady asked very professionally.

"They're both with me," Bruce said, stepping closer to them.

The woman continued. "This was some of the best, if not the best, singing we have heard in this mall competition. In two weeks we are having a larger competition at the Woodfield Mall. The first place winner there gets one thousand dollars and moves on to our final competition which is nationwide. The winner of that competition will sign with a top record label. Neither of you should miss this. Here is my number. Call me, and I will get you a spot for the contest, which is coming up in two weeks."

Jonathan and Dominique were so excited that they gave each other a hug. They pulled away, somewhat embarrassed but no big deal; it was just part of the moment.

After a moment, Jonathan's excitement faded because he had to face reality. "This ain't gonna work. My father will never let me do this."

"Now don't talk like that. I will speak with him and inform him of how awesome you did and how the crowd responded. Trust me, he will let you sing," Bruce said with confidence.

"You really think so?" Jonathan asked, allowing himself to smile again.

"I will give it my best," Bruce said with confidence.

Chapter
Eleven

What About Stitch
and Double K?

Finally, after a day of excitement, they left the mall and made their way toward the train to get back to their part of town.

"I didn't know you could sing like that," Josh commented to Jonathan.

"What was that little rap in the middle of the song? I never heard anyone do that before," Dominique said, delivering a complimentary gesture.

"I just feel certain things at times during a song, and I like to try them when the pressure is on. I've already written forty-two songs, but every time I talk to my dad about them he comes back with a negative comment."

"Like what?" Bruce asked curiously.

"Like...'everybody wants to be a singer' and 'that dream is far fetched.' You know...stuff like that," Jonathan answered. He turned his head after hearing his name called from a distance.

He looked over to see Stitch, Double K and a few of the guys waving him over.

Jonathan looked at Bruce, Dominique and Josh. He

had not only a guilty look on his face but also a look as if he had almost forgotten about those guys after all that had happened that day.

"Give me a second. I'll be right back," Jonathan said as he took off toward them.

"Dad, aren't you going to stop him? He's your responsibility, isn't he?" Dominique asked with great concern.

"Give him his space. Let's see what he's going to do. I can't make his decisions for him," Mr. Galardi said, knowing his job as a police officer very well.

Jonathan arrived at where the guys were standing.

"What's up?" Jonathan questioned.

"Tomorrow, we meet at Millers Chevrolet. They just got in a new batch of Corvettes, and we are going to do a number on them," Stitch said with a high five to Double K.

"Listen, guys, there has been a change of plans on my part. I made a bad decision, and I'm pulling out on everything. I suggest you do the same. You can't live this life and follow your dreams at the same time," Jonathan said with wisdom.

"What do you mean, you're out?" Double K asked.

"What are these dreams you are talking about? I don't have any dreams," Stitch said, a little aggravated.

"And you never will if you keep on doing this kind of stuff," Jonathan responded as he headed back to his three friends.

Stitch, Double K and the rest of the gang just watched him go.

"We can't just let him off like that," Double K said.

"That's right. He knows too much, and he could rat us out," Stitch agreed as he formulated a devious plan in his mind.

When Jonathan arrived back with his friends, Josh questioned him immediately.

"What did they want?" Josh asked, knowing it would

not be a good thing.

"Not much," Jonathan said, answering so they could all hear. He then continued proudly: "I told them I had made a change of plans, and I would no longer be hanging with them. I suggested that they do the same."

"Good, I'm proud of you." Bruce said with a smile.

Jonathan stopped for a moment and just stared at Bruce, taking in that comment. He never heard anyone say that they were proud of him. It felt good, and he wanted to enjoy the moment.

They continued walking, but Mr. Galardi could hear Adam in his ear.

"Mr. Galardi, can you hear me?" Adam said from back at the Zone.

Mr. Galardi let Dominique, Josh and Jonathan get a few steps ahead of him before he answered. "I hear you loud and clear, Adam."

"Are you thinking what we're thinking back here?" Adam asked.

"That we are not going to see the last of Stitch and his buddies, and that trouble awaits for Jonathan? If that's what you're thinking, then yes," Mr. Galardi replied.

"That's what we're thinking," Adam responds for the whole team.

"What can we do?" Mr. Galardi asked, wondering if Adam had any gadgets for this situation.

"For now, we can follow his whereabouts and alert you if he approaches Jonathan," Adam responded in a professional manner.

"Can you tell if any of them are carrying guns?" Mr.

Galardi questioned. He knew if they were carrying guns they could be following them and attack from a distance.

Adam responded quickly, "Mr. Galardi, they are clean in the gun department. However, Stitch seems to be carrying a blade of some sort hidden on the lower part of his right leg."

"All right, Adam, that's—" Mr. Galardi was interrupted by Adam.

"Hold on, sir," Adam said as he paused a moment, then continued. "Two males are approaching Jonathan, Dominique and Josh. I almost have a clear view of who they are...Yep, it's not Stitch or Double K, it's two of their other guys. Hold on, Mr. Galardi, let me warn Josh. 'Josh, do you read me? If you do, you have trouble approaching about ten feet on your left.'"

"I see them, Adam. Where is Mr. Galardi?" Josh asked with some concern, putting his hand over his mouth so Jonathan couldn't hear him talk.

"He's coming up behind you," Adam responded.

Mr. Galardi interjected, "Adam, tell them to hang tight and let these guys say what they have to say. I'm right behind them, and I can see everything that is going on. Tell Dominique and Josh to not panic." Mr. Galardi hung back several feet behind the action.

"Did you copy that, Dominique and Josh? Nod your heads if you did," Adam instructed.

They both nodded. Very calmly, Josh alerted Jonathan of the intruders approaching on his left.

"Hey, man, we have company," Josh said, looking to his left.

93

Jonathan stopped and waited to see what they wanted.

As the two approached, Jonathan questioned them. "What's up guys? I thought I told you I wouldn't be hanging with you all."

"We thought we'd give you a second chance to change your mind;" one kid said, sporting a cocky attitude.

"Thanks, but no thanks. I made my mind up, and I'm not going to change it," Jonathan said, standing firm.

"Is this your girlfriend? She's pretty," the second thug said to Jonathan, referring to Dominique. He continued, "I'd hate to see anything happen to her. You know what I'm saying?"

Hearing everything that was going on, Mr. Galardi came running up from behind as if he didn't know what was taking place.

"Hey, you guys. We'd better hurry up if we don't want to miss the train," Mr. Galardi said. "Oh, are these some of you guys' friends?" he asked in his Bruce character. He extended his hand to the bigger of the two street kids.

They both just looked at Mr. Galardi with an attitude. The bigger one extended his hand to keep Bruce from having any suspicions about what had just been said.

When they shook hands, Mr. Galardi introduced himself with a smile and a grip in his handshake that could crush a diamond. "Hi, I'm Bruce. What's your name?"

The kid was in so much pain from Mr. Galardi's tight-grip handshake that he couldn't even concentrate on the question that was just asked of him.

Mr. Galardi kept gripping tighter and smiling bigger. The kid figured that if he answered the question the vice-like grip of the handshake would be over.

"Tailgate," the kid said. "My name is Tailgate."

"Tailgate," Mr. Galardi repeated, looking at the other guy. He questioned him. "What kind of name is that? What is your name?"

"Bumper," he replied.

Mr. Galardi began to laugh. "I'm just kidding. That must be a nickname."

"They call me Tailgate because I'm the last thing you see as I back up into you."

Keeping it light and goofy, Mr. Galardi continued. "Well, that's a good thing to know. Good thing for me, I don't have a car. But if I get one, I'll look out for you. It was nice meeting you boys. We gotta go, or we're going to miss our train," Mr. Galardi added and then just walked away before they could say anything else.

Tailgate and his friend just stood there and watched them walk off. They were thrown off by Mr. Galardi's goofy character, but they just didn't get it.

"Those guys were harassing us," Dominique said to her dad.

"Yeah, well the best thing to do is make light of it and move on," Mr. Galardi said with a smile as he continued to walk.

Dominique and Josh got the hint that he wanted to drop the subject until later.

"C'mon you guys. Hurry, or we are going to miss this train, and the next one doesn't come for twenty-five minutes," Mr. Galardi said as he started to run.

Dominique, Josh and Jonathan followed after him, and

they all made it onto the train before the doors closed.

They found seats across from each other so they could talk. This was good because the ride home was about forty-five minutes long.

Jonathan began the conversation. "So, Bruce, you sure you're going to talk to my dad about the singing thing?"

"I told you I would. I will, but not tonight though." Mr. Galardi answered

"How about tomorrow?" Jonathan said, excited about his dream possibly becoming a reality.

"Tomorrow, I promise," Mr. Galardi said with a smile.

Mr. Galardi looked out the window and thought about what he had to do to handle the Stitch situation when it came up.

Chapter
Twelve

Mr. Galardi Has
His Hands Full

Mr. Galardi, Dominique, Josh and Monica were back at the hotel having a meeting with the Fighting Chance team via the computer's audio and visual capabilities.

"I am a little worried, Dad." Dominique said.

"Worried about what, Dominique...that they threatened you or that they called you Jonathan's girlfriend?" DJ said from back at the Zone.

Everyone chuckled at that comment, and Dominique's face slowly turned three shades of red.

"Jonathan is kind of cute," Kelly said in response.

"Yeah, if you like the karate chop kind of guy," Billy added with a sarcastic tone.

Before the word game could continue, Mr. Galardi threw out a question from out of the blue.

"Hey, Adam, whatever happened to my bike?"

Monica had to respond to that comment. "Well, I'm glad that last little bit of memory has come back, Joseph...or is it Bruce? What would you like me to call you?" Monica said with a smile as she threw her arms around her husband and gave him a kiss on the cheek.

Adam answered in his professional tone, "Don't worry about your bike. When Josh returned...before he returned with you, he brought it back with him. We have it here with us. It does have a few minor scratches on it, but other than that it looks perfect."

"Thanks, guys, again I'm very proud of all of you. Now let's concentrate on Dominique and her threatening, yet traumatizing, situation," Mr. Galardi said.

Adam had had time to think about that situation and, as always, had a perfect answer. "Josh, if you will look in the black bag, there is a ring box. Grab that if you will."

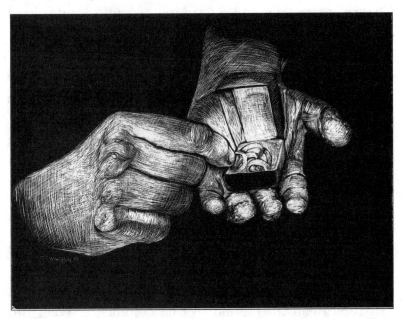

Josh reached into the bag and pulled out the ring box. He opened it and found several silver rings in the bottom.

"What are these for?" Josh asked, completely confused.

Adam began to explain to all of them what to do. "You

guys will find these rings both comforting and interesting. Furthermore, there are no rings like these anywhere in the world."

"There is no one like you anywhere in the world." Jackie said in her sarcastic, joking way.

Adam just gave her a look as the rest laughed. Then he continued, "As I was saying... Dominique, one ring is for you and the other is for Josh. Since both of you are right handed, place them on your right hand on the finger that it fits best."

The two of them placed the rings on their best fitting finger.

"Now what?" Dominique asked.

"Now you are protected," Adam said as he continued. "These rings have two functions: One is somewhat dangerous and the other is completely harmless. They send a very high-powered shock wave through the bad guy, so to say, which could be dangerous. Through the process of elimination, I have perfected this device to be useful, yet not as dangerous. When striking your opponents, it can send a horrible pain throughout their bodies while at the same time not harm them at all. If you are in a dangerous situation, then you can use the electrical shock which will knock them out for a while and may cause serious harm, but it won't kill anyone." Adam explained.

Adam added, "Dominique and Josh, if you are wondering how the rings are activated, that's what I am so excited about. I just finished this invention before I met all of you. I was hoping we would have a chance to use them. They are voice-activated. If you say 'Strike,' they will be effective and somewhat harmless to your opponent. If you say 'Shock,' they will be put down for a while. Remember, they will not work until your voice activates them. We can do that in a minute. After this mission I will upgrade them, and they will pick up on the nerve waves in your body and transfer from strike to shock just by your thought process. Pretty cool, huh?" Adam said as the rest of the Gang shook their heads.

Mr. Galardi looked over at Monica and smiled. This was her first time experiencing this kind of genius.

"Mr. Galardi, if the mission takes much longer and you feel you are not in any danger, we can bring Monica back and then transport her and your other two children so that you can all be together," Adam suggested.

"Maybe, we'll see," Mr. Galardi responded.

The Next Afternoon

As the parents dropped off their kids for the afternoon karate class, some of them stayed to watch, but some just dropped off their kids and left.

Monica had brought Dominique and Josh. She was sitting in the watch area while Dominique was talking to Jonathan. Actually, she wasn't really talking to him; she was singing and showing him a new song she was writing. He loved talking about music and began to give her some very helpful suggestions pertaining to the creative parts of the song.

Mr. Galardi walked past Monica, and winked at her as he made his way toward Nick's office.

After a soft knock on the door, Nick invited him in.

Mr. Galardi walked up to Nick's desk and posed a question to the ever-so-stern Nick Anderson.

"Mr. Anderson, may I talk with you for a moment?"

"Sure, Bruce, take a seat," Nick said, somewhat preoccupied.

Not knowing what to expect from him, Mr. Galardi gave it to him straight.

"Yesterday, I took three kids from here to the mall. One of them was your son."

"Yeah, thanks. He told me that he had a good time and that you wanted to talk to me about something," Nick answered, finally giving Mr. Galardi his full attention.

"Your son got up on stage and sang in a mall competition. He won second place. The crowd went wild for him." Mr. Galardi said excitedly.

"Sorry I missed it," Nick commented, with little to no enthusiasm.

"He has been invited to go further. The promotional tour manager at the mall feels that he has as good a chance as any to win the entire competition, which, in this case, is a recording contract." Mr. Galardi said not knowing how Nick would respond.

Nick rubbed his hand across his face. Taking a deep breath, he answered, "Is there anything else you need?"

"No, I just thought it would be a great confidence booster for Jonathan, with everything he's been through," Mr. Galardi said, waiting for an unpleasant comment from Nick.

"Thank you for the information. This afternoon is our open spar class. We'll be having some very important guests joining us this evening. I'll need you to help out as much as possible where needed," Nick said, letting Mr. Galardi know that the conversation about Jonathan was over.

"No problem, Mr. Anderson. What is an 'open spar' class?" Mr. Galardi asked, knowing fully what it was.

"It's when we invite other schools to join us in point fighting. It gives us all a chance to express our talents. To be honest with you, other schools are always in friendly competition with us, and this gives us a chance to remind them who is the best," Mr. Anderson said as he winked at Mr. Galardi. "Plus, we have some investors who may be interested in putting money up for me to open several other schools in the Chicago area."

"Yes, sir. I'll do my best to help out," Mr. Galardi said respectfully.

Nick and Mr. Galardi both walked out of the door. Mr. Galardi walked over to Monica, and Nick called his son Jonathan.

Jonathan excused himself from Dominique, and with great excitement ran to his father's office.

Jonathan closed the door behind him and waited. He hoped for good news.

"Yes, sir," he said to his father.

"I understand you won some little competition in the mall yesterday," Nick said.

With a smile, Jonathan answered, "Yes, sir, I did."

"Congratulations! Are you ready to take your training a little more seriously now that you have had a little fun?" Nick addressed him sternly.

"Of course," Jonathan said as he continued. "Does this mean I can enter the next level of competition at the Woodfield Mall?" Jonathan asked respectfully yet excitedly.

Nick did not like how Jonathan's love for singing was greater than that of karate.

"No! And I will hear no more about this singing garbage. I am the best in this sport of martial arts, and I am raising my children to follow in my footsteps. I am a world champion competitive fighter, not a lollygagging stage singer. My sons will be world champions as well. Do I make myself clear to you, son?" Nick said with no room for arguing.

Jonathan, very disappointed, took a moment to hold back his tears from yet another putdown by his father. "Yes, sir."

"Has anyone ever been able to beat me, son?" Nick asked, trying to prove a point.

"No, sir," Jonathan answered with his head down.

"That's because I work hard at what I do. You will do the same. That will be all." Nick instructed as he looked down and began to work on some papers on his desk.

Jonathan walked out the office, and didn't say a word to anyone.

Mr. Galardi looked at his wife. They could tell from the look on Jonathan's face that it didn't go very well.

Josh and Dominique ran up to Monica to hand her their rings. They were not allowed to wear them in karate class.

"Mom, make sure you don't mix them up. They are already voice activated to our voices," Dominique said respectfully.

The class had been going on for about thirty minutes, and Nick Anderson was full of smiles because all of his students were winning in the sparring matches.

Nick had his protective fighting gear on and had been sparring with the instructors from the other schools. They were really no competition for Nick, and the smiles on the investors' faces showed that they understood that Nick Anderson was clearly the best.

The other instructors commented how much they appreciated that Nick Anderson sparred with them and taught them new techniques that would better their abilities.

"Again, Mr. Anderson, thank you for the opportunity to be able to spar with you. I have learned a lot this afternoon, and I will be able to take this knowledge back to my school," one instructor and owner from another school commented.

Nick wouldn't let Jonathan spar because he was afraid that he would embarrass him by losing. Jonathan has been sitting next to Dominique, and they were talking music as much as possible without getting caught by his father.

Nick had just finished beating another opponent and removed his mouthpiece to question the group. "Would anyone else like to go at it? We are just about out of time."

There were no takers, so Jonathan spoke up. "Why don't you spar Bruce? He hasn't gotten a chance."

Nick smiled, thinking that Jonathan couldn't be serious.

A few of the other kids chimed in. "C'mon, Mr.

Anderson, give Bruce a chance."

Nick looked over at his son Kevin to see what he thought. Kevin smiled and nodded to his father that he should give Bruce a chance.

"All right, why not. Bruce, you want to give it a try?" Nick asked.

"Me?" Bruce asked, pointing to himself. He was embarrassed.

Bruce casually looked over at his wife, and she gave him a subtle nod.

In a silly goofy way, Bruce agreed. "Well, OK, I'll give it a shot."

"Jonathan, maybe you can help Bruce get some protective gear on," Nick instructed his son.

Nick began talking to his investors, and Mr. Galardi went over to Jonathan to get suited up.

Mr. Galardi was not in a karate gee; he was dressed in sweat pants and a big shirt.

Jonathan began to hand Mr. Galardi the protective fighting gear so that he could prepare for the match with his father.

"All right, why are you doing this to me?" Mr. Galardi asked.

"I'm not trying to get back at you or anything, I just want you to get a first hand feel of how miserable it is to be intimidated by him." Jonathan said as he helped Bruce put on the last piece of protective fighting gear.

Jonathan's parting words were, "Don't worry, he won't hurt you too badly."

"Thanks for the encouraging word," Mr. Galardi said.

Then he made his way to the center, where the sparring match would take place.

Nick explained to Mr. Galardi the basic rules. "All right, Bruce. The target areas where you can receive points are the head and the body. You can't hit in the back, and you can't hit the legs. Understand?" Nick asked, then explained to those in the viewing area who included his potential investors. "Bruce has come to us by accident. He has temporary amnesia and has been a great help to us here at the school. He's somewhat familiar with the martial arts but he isn't sure how much he knows." Nick said jokingly as everyone laughed, including Bruce.

Dominique looked over at Josh. They just smiled at each other.

Adam and the Fighting Chance team didn't want to miss out on the action. They were keeping a close watch on the big screen back at the Zone.

Nick instructed his son Kevin to referee the match. "OK, Bruce, are you ready?"

"Ready as I'll ever be, I guess," Bruce answered, all shy and humble.

Kevin began the match, and the two fighters moved around the square fighting ring that was marked on the floor.

Nick threw a kick, and Bruce blocked it. He struck back with a short jab to the head so fast that Nick didn't see it coming.

"Break," Kevin said. He continued, "One point for Bruce."

The kids cheered.

Nick smiled, knowing he had to take this more seriously.

Bruce settled in and waited for something from Nick. Nick demonstrated a combination of kicks and punches, trying to score on Bruce, but he failed again. Bruce countered with a jab to the head and a front kick to the stomach followed by a few body punches.

"Break," Kevin announced, as he awarded another point to Bruce.

Bruce began to smile and put his hands down as if to show Nick that he didn't really have to try.

Nick was getting frustrated. He decided to move aggressively toward Bruce. Bruce blocked everything Nick threw, then swept Nick off his feet and threw him to the ground, tagging him for another point.

"Three points for Bruce; none for Mr. Anderson," Kevin said professionally.

Jonathan just stared at the situation. He couldn't believe what he was seeing. Jonathan was sure that his father was just letting Bruce win.

"You're letting me get points aren't you, Mr. Anderson?" Bruce said, trying to get Nick to try harder.

Nick nodded his head, knowing that he was giving his very best.

"I thought so, because this is too easy," Mr. Galardi said.

"Do you want to feel what it's really like to be in ring competition?" Nick asked Bruce.

"Yes, sir, Mr. Anderson. Give me all you've got," Bruce respectfully answered.

Nick lunged toward Bruce with a very sleek move, which Bruce easily blocked. He threw a very fast round kick, tapping Nick in the head for another easy point.

The match continued, and Bruce kept gaining one point after another, not allowing Nick to get even one point.

The score was ten to nothing, and Jonathan was speechless. The kids back at the Zone were cheering as if this were a professional boxing match.

Nick gave Bruce every punch and kick he had, trying to land at least one point before the match was over. Bruce blocked them all and threw one punch to the stomach. The punch was so hard that Nick got the wind knocked out of him. He dropped to the floor on one knee and removed his mouthpiece. He signaled with his hand that the match was over.

The kids were cheering for Bruce, and the adults stood there confused, not understanding why this had happened. For ten years straight Nick had never been beaten...until today.

Bruce made his way over to Nick and extended his hand to help him up. "Good fight, Mr. Anderson," Bruce respectfully said.

"Well done, Bruce," Nick said, as he made his way to the head of the class.

Nick ended the class, then made his way toward his office. He motioned for Bruce to join him in just a minute. Nick said good-bye to his investors. They would talk further about opening new schools. They liked Nick Anderson and were serious about moving ahead as planned.

Jonathan walked up to Bruce. "What in the world was all that about? No one has ever beaten my dad. You were right. There is always somebody better out there. Today he met him. Wow!" Jonathan was stunned.

Monica motioned to Bruce that Nick was waiting for him.

Bruce made his way to the office and closed the door behind him.

"Do you realize how it feels to be humiliated like I just was out there?" Nick remarked to Bruce.

Before Bruce could answer, Nick asked again. "Do you even know how that feels?"

Nick just stared at Bruce.

"No, sir, but I'm sure Jonathan does," Bruce answered respectfully, proving a point.

Nick paused for a while as the answer to his question sunk in. "Oh my gosh...I had no idea...That poor kid. This is how I made him feel."

Nick put his head in his hand and again looked up at Bruce. "Who are you? Even if you are skilled in the martial arts I have never heard nor seen of you. This should not have happened to me. I didn't even get one point, and I gave you everything I had."

"May I speak freely, Mr. Anderson?" Bruce asked.

"Please, say anything you like," Nick added.

"The sparring match meant nothing to me, and it should've meant nothing to you. Your son is crushed on the inside and has been crying out for your attention, only to be shot down every time he doesn't meet up to your standards. His dreams are not your dreams, and he will never be able to operate fully in the gifts he has if he is forced to operate in the ones you want him to have. He will grow and become a better martial artist as he gets older, but he is a great singer now. Can you imagine the incredible joy that he is missing because he is forced to better himself in your gifts rather than the ones that were meant just for him? Support him in his singing, and you will see him grow in all areas. I mean really support him. Make it a great interest of yours so he can see that you are behind him, and if he wins his singing competition then you praise him. If he loses then you can encourage him that you are standing behind him to become the very best he can be. Like I said to him a few days ago, 'You can be the best there is, but someday someone better comes along. That doesn't mean you quit. That means you try harder.'"

Nick just looked at Bruce. "I don't know who you are or where you come from, but how can I ever thank you?"

"Don't worry about thanking me. Just worry about getting Jonathan to be the best singer he can be. Are you aware that he has written forty-two songs?"

There was a short pause on Nick's part.

"You two have a lot of catching up to do. Trust me, it's going to be awesome," Bruce said with a kind, comforting smile.

"Bruce, can you do me a favor? When you go in the back could you send Jonathan up here to my office?"

"Sure,." Bruce said, as Adam interrupted him.

"Mr. Galardi! Get to the back of the building ASAP! Stitch and his boys are on their way, and it doesn't seem peaceful. Dominique and Josh are sitting back there talking, and they are going to be the first ones they get to. Do you copy?"

"Yes! I copy that, Mr. Anderson. I'll tell Jonathan you would like to see him right away," Bruce said, answering Adam but using Mr. Anderson as a cover-up.

Chapter
Thirteen

A Dangerous Situation
to Face

Mr. Galardi quickly walked out of the office only to see Monica sitting alone. The rest of the parents had left, and there was no one left in the place.

"Monica, where are the kids?" Mr. Galardi asked, a little stressed over the situation.

She answered, "Josh and Dominique came and got their rings. They said they were going with Jonathan to the back workout area."

Mr. Galardi stopped immediately to focus and concentrate on what Adam was saying in his ear. "Go ahead, Adam, I read you loud and clear."

"We have a situation here, Mr. Galardi. The back door of the karate school is open. Oh, man, this isn't good. Four guys are right outside the . . . Get back there right away! They have Dominique and Josh at knife-point. They have no guns. Three more carloads of people are about to pull up. Do you want me to contact the Chicago PD?"

Mr. Galardi was almost at the back door. "I'm just about there. Hold on the Chicago PD, and keep me aware of everything that's happening. Are their guns in the cars?

Anything unusual? I need to know everything."

"Yes, sir, Mr. Galardi, we are right on it," Adam responded.

Mr. Galardi came running out the back door, only to find Josh and Dominique at knifepoint and Jonathan just watching in complete fear. Josh and Dominique did not seem to be very worried, considering the circumstances.

Ten more kids exited the three vehicles and started walking towards the action.

"This is not good, man." Stitch said to Jonathan. He continued, "What's he doing here?" Stitch was anxiously concerned about Mr. Galardi's presence, almost panic-stricken.

"What are you guys doing?" Mr. Galardi asked, continuing. "Stitch and Double K. Did I get it right? Two guys who have never been in real trouble who now face a great criminal charge unless you put those knifes down. What's it going to be?"

Stitch and Double K just looked at Mr. Galardi, not knowing what their immediate reaction should be.

Stitch put his knife down at his side, and Double K just looked at him. "What're you doing?" Double K questioned.

"What does it look like I'm doing? I'm putting my knife down. What are you doing?"

Double K gave Stitch a goofy look. "Same thing," Double K says as he dropped his knife.

"What're you guys doing? Don't listen to him," one of the kids called out.

"And why shouldn't they listen to me? I'm giving them a chance to make the right decision rather than the one you are about to make." Mr. Galardi said, trying to help the kid understand.

This kid was about twenty-two years old, and he didn't want to accept Mr. Galardi's offer. He began walking toward Mr. Galardi not only with anger, but also with the intention of doing something.

"He's pulling a knife on you. Be careful," Adam said to Mr. Galardi.

The twenty-two year-old kid was named "Tailgate." That's the kid Mr. Galardi met at the train station.

Tailgate stopped just before Mr. Galardi, and instead of going after him, he grabbed Dominique and began to threaten her.

"I told you I would be the last thing you see as I back into you. Who is this little lady? It's a shame she has to suffer because you stuck your nose into our business," Tailgate said to Mr. Galardi, then directed a comment to Stitch. "I got your back, Stitch."

"Are you sure this is what you want to do?" Mr. Galardi asked of Tailgate.

"Man, don't try to negotiate with me," Tailgate said as a final answer.

"Shock or strike?" Dominique asked her dad.

Mr. Galardi was so relaxed as he answered the question. "Ah, let's see. I would say strike. Yeah, that should do it."

"Strike!" Dominique announced as she took the order and slapped her right hand onto Tailgate's right leg.

Nothing happened. Both Dominique and Mr. Galardi were in shock.

"Little girl, don't try and defend yourself against me.

That karate stuff doesn't work on us big boys," Tailgate said as he laughed at the slapping situation.

"You guys switched rings," Adam said in their earpieces and then continued. "You are close enough, Josh, just call out 'Strike' and her ring will be activated."

Dominique nodded to Josh that she was ready, and Josh nodded back. Without wasting any more time, Josh called out the code, "Strike!"

Dominique again slapped her hand on Tailgate's leg. This time he fell to the ground and began screaming because he was in great pain.

The ring caused his leg muscles to completely cramp up, causing such great pain that he cried like a little baby who didn't get his bottle in time.

The cramping only lasted for sixty seconds. Any longer and the human body couldn't handle it.

After a minute the cramping stopped. Tailgate, with tears in his eyes, stood to his feet and took a few steps, limping.

"I guess you backed into a tree this time, didn't you?" Mr. Galardi said with a smile on his face.

"I wasn't going to hurt her. I was just going scare you," Tailgate said fearfully.

"Once you take action, you have to be ready to receive the consequences," Mr. Galardi said to Tailgate. He then continued, speaking to all of them. "We are not here to call the cops on you guys. We don't want to see your lives destroyed before you can even begin. Hang tight for a second, will you? Stitch, can I speak with you for a minute?"

Stitch walked over to Mr. Galardi. As they walked a few steps away from the crowd, Mr. Galardi began to speak in a soft, low voice so the rest of them couldn't hear him.

"Stitch! Let's see, that's the kind of name you give yourself when you're in a car wreck and your father is holding you together to save your life and in the process loses his. Is this how you repay the man who loved you enough to give his own life? Would this make your father proud of you?"

"How do you know about my father?" Stitch asked.

Adam interrupted with further information. "Mr. Galardi, Stitch's mother got married a year and a half after his fathers death. There have been two domestic violence cases reported. Stitch and his stepfather apparently don't get along very well."

Mr. Galardi continued, "It's not important how I know about your father. Your mother married your stepfather a year and a half after your father's death, and you were not happy with that so you took it out on your stepfather and your mother. Let me finish before you answer. I realize it's hard to lose a loved one, and it's OK to be sad; it's not OK to take it out on yourself. The bad decisions you are making are because you are angry that your father died."

"You don't understand. My stepfather is a big jerk," Stitch answered angrily.

"What makes him a big jerk?" Mr. Galardi asked.

Stitch thought for a moment, but didn't really have an answer. Tears began to well up in his eyes, and he tried to hold back his feelings.

"There really is no answer, is there? Your stepfather can't just fill the shoes of your real father, and it seems that you take out a lot of your anger on your stepfather. Could that possibly be how it is?" Mr. Galardi asked very compassionately.

"I don't know, maybe," Stitch answered, all confused.

Nick Anderson came out of the back door of his building and was concerned about what was going on.

"What's the problem, Jonathan?" Nick asked.

"We're having a little situation here," Mr. Galardi said as he continued. "This is how I see it. There are fourteen of you here right now. There are three cars, and I have the license plate numbers right now."

Back at the Zone, Adam picked up on Mr. Galardi's comment and zoomed in on the plates. He ran a complete information check on them. "I'm on it, Mr. Galardi. Keep talking, and I'll feed you the info in just a moment."

Mr. Galardi continued without a break. "Seven of you are carrying knives, and three of you held these two young people at knifepoint, threatening their lives. Tomorrow at 10:30 A.M. you will be here in this exact spot, and I will give you further instructions as to what is going to happen. If you all return, we will not prosecute, however, if even one of you is missing; we will prosecute all of you. Do I make myself clear?" Mr. Galardi said, as Adam came through, giving him the information he needed. Mr. Galardi continued to blow their minds and scare the bad right out of them. "Ron Stutter, you own that blue Mazda, license plate number BAD-1. You have two traffic violations, and you still owe $4,357.28 on that car. Rafael Sanchez, you own the red Chevy Malibu license plate RD-BST. This car is registered in your parent's name, and they still owe $3,742.32. One more traffic violation, and your license will be revoked. Leon Vargo, you own the gold metallic Mustang. It's paid for, and you have no traffic violations. It seems that you are a pretty good kid, but you want to shake the goodie-two-shoes attitude and do something bad. Not a good idea. Would you like me to inform you further that we will find you if you don't show up tomorrow?"

They all agreed to be there as Mr. Galardi asked.

"And by the way, let's call off the Miller Chevrolet deal you had going this evening. Sound good to you?" Mr. Galardi added with complete authority.

"Yeah, we figured that was a bad idea anyway. Right guys?" Stitch commented.

Double K was in such awe that Mr. Galardi knew all that information about him. "How did you..."

Mr. Galardi cut him off. "Don't worry. Just be here tomorrow at 10:30 A.M."

They just nodded their heads, slowly walked back to their cars and took off.

Mr. Galardi looked over at Nick and saw that Nick was in a state of confusion.

"Mr. Anderson, we need to talk," Mr. Galardi said.

"That would be a good idea. Can we do it now, please?" Nick requested.

"As a matter of fact, we can all talk, I mean Jonathan, Josh, Dominique—all of us. Is that OK with all of you?" Mr. Galardi suggested.

Chapter
Fourteen

Things Are Looking Up

Nick Anderson, Jonathan, Josh, Dominique and Bruce, AKA Mr. Galardi were all walking back to the main room. Nick instructed them to have a seat on the floor.

Mr. Galardi motioned for Monica to come and join them. He took a seat on the floor and leaned his head back against the wall, took a deep breath, and released it all at once. After a short pause, he began to fill in the blanks. In other words, he began to explain the whole story...well, not the whole story. He couldn't tell anyone about the Fighting Chance team, the Zone, or the transporter or any of that stuff.

"When you found me that day, right outside that window over there, I had slipped on the wet grass and hit my head on a rock of some sort. Like the doctor said, I had amnesia. How and when my memory would return was to be determined only with time.

"A few days ago, I realized who I was. It came back to me just as fast as it left. Monica is my wife, and Dominique is my daughter. Josh is just a friend. Once they found out what happened to me, they came here to try to help me remember who I was. Well, they did a great job. My name is not Bruce Lee, of course. It's Joseph Galardi, and I am a detective. The reason we didn't leave right away is because of this gang situation with Jonathan. We have an organization that helps kids before they get sent to juvenile hall.

That's why I asked all those kids to return here tomorrow morning at 10:30. This is where you come in, Mr. Anderson."

"Wait a minute. This is unbelievable. You just saved my son's life and—"

Mr. Galardi cut in. "No, I just gave Jonathan the two situations. He made the right decision and chose the right road."

"Hold on a second," Nick said to the group as he got up and ran into his office.

After a moment, Nick returned with a small scrapbook. He began to fumble through the pages and stopped on one of them, placing his finger in the book to save the spot while he continued to talk. "Did you say your name is Joseph Galardi?"

"Yes, why do you ask?" Mr. Galardi requested.

Nick opened the book and showed Mr. Galardi a signed picture in his scrapbook. The picture was taken from a kick boxing match about three years ago.

"Could you possibly be the same Joseph Galardi who signed this picture about three years ago after becoming the national kick boxing champion?" Nick asked with a smile on his face, hoping he was correct.

Joseph Galardi took a moment to decide whether or not he wanted to answer that question. He realized that even though some things had to remain a secret, that didn't have to be one of them.

He answered while nodding his head, "Yes, I am that same Joseph Galardi."

Nick and Jonathan just stood there in awe. It had been a lot of information for them to swallow in a few short minutes.

"I want to thank you for helping me when I was suffering my memory loss," Joseph Galardi added. He continued, "You're a good family. What you did for me, you didn't have to do, but you welcomed me without question. Instead of prosecuting the boys who are coming tomorrow, I would like to suggest that they train under your organization for six months—free classes of course—and follow your instructions and morals for taking the right path. Those boys, and boys like them, need guidance; they need to feel a sense of accomplishment and—"

Nick interrupted, "Say no more. It's done. Whatever you suggest, I will do."

Joseph Galardi added some words of wisdom. "Mr. Anderson, you will gain more respect by helping those in need than you will by becoming a bigger champion. You've already made it. Now it's time to help give others a fighting chance."

"I've never lost a match that has allowed me to win at the same time," Nick said, as he took a moment. He truly understood everything Joseph Galardi had just told him. Nick smiled, looked at Jonathan, and began to speak from his heart. "Son, you did your best at the tournament last week. I guess I came down a little hard on you. It's my job to make sure you become the best. I want you to become the best at what you are gifted in, not what I am gifted in. Do you know what I need you to do?" Nick asked as he waited for an answer.

"No, what?" Jonathan answered, completely unaware of what his father was about to say.

Nick instructed him in his stern fashion. "I need you to give me your best, and I need you to work as hard as you can. I want to see you do the best you possibly can when you enter that singing competition at the Woodfield Mall next week."

Jonathan smiled with tears in his eyes. He couldn't believe his father just said what he did. Jonathan looked over at Dominique, then to Mr. Galardi, then ran over to his father and threw his arms around him.

Nick grabbed hold of Jonathan and hugged him so tight...like he never planned to let him go.

"I'm sorry, son. I almost lost you because of my selfish ways. Your mother tried to tell me about your singing, and I wouldn't listen to her. When we get home, let's take the whole family to dinner and inform them of your new path."

Nick looked up at Joseph Galardi. "Would you like to join us?"

"I think your family has a lot to talk about and a lot of planning to do. Maybe we can join you at another time." Joseph Galardi answered

The serious moment was somewhat broken when they looked over at Dominique and saw her crying with her hands clenched over her mouth. "I just love happy endings," she said in a high squeaky voice.

"Dad, you should hear her sing. She's the one who came in first last week," Jonathan added. He looked puzzled.

"What's that look for?" Dominique commented, then continued "It looks like you have gas or something."

Everyone laughed.

"No, I don't have gas. I was just wondering, Dominique, now that all this is all in the open, are you still going to enter the competition at the Woodfield Mall?"

Dominique looked at her dad and mom because that was a question she couldn't answer.

"Dominique, I think you should stay and give it a try. Besides, it will allow us to hang around and help Mr. Anderson with these fourteen kids who are starting class tomorrow," Joseph Galardi said.

Everyone stood, and Nick Anderson shook hands with Joseph. "If there is anything you need during your stay here in Chicago, don't hesitate to ask."

"Thanks. I won't need to stay in the back room anymore. I think I'll hang with my wife and family for the remainder of our stay here," Joseph Galardi said with a smile.

"Oh, look at Mr. Galardi...all cool now that the day is saved and he's hanging with the fam." DJ said back at the Zone.

"I heard that, DJ." Mr. Galardi said aloud in front of everyone.

"Kelly, you forget to turn off the transmit button again," DJ said.

"Who's DJ?," Jonathan asked Mr. Galardi.

Quick on his feet, Mr. Galardi answered. "I heard that DJ at the hotel plays some good music, so that's where we are headed. Right, my wonderful family?"

Dominique, Monica and Josh all laughed because they heard the goof up from DJ back at the Zone.

Chapter
Fifteen

A Second FIGHTING CHANCE TEAM
Forms in Chicago

The next morning, 10:30 appeared to be very early for the fourteen young men. Stitch and his boys were just in time. They didn't look very happy, but they are on time and ready to go.

There were several undercover police officers in the karate school who were going to pose as temporary instructors.

The fourteen kids were lounging on the floor. Some of them were sleeping against the wall, and some were actually laying on the floor with their jackets pulled over their heads. It didn't look like a promising bunch.

Everything that Mr. Galardi had told Stitch yesterday about his father must have really touched Stitch's heart, because when Joseph entered the room Stitch went over to him and greeted him with a handshake.

Stitch couldn't wait to bring Joseph over to meet his mother and stepfather. "Would you come with me? I want you to meet my family," Stitch said as he led Mr. Galardi to where his parents were sitting.

Entering the waiting area, Stitch introduced Joseph to his parents. "Mr. Galardi, this is my mother, Jan Matos, and this is my stepfather, Andrew Matos."

Joseph responded respectfully by shaking their hands. "It's a pleasure to meet both of you."

Jan Matos got tears in her eyes as she spoke to Joseph. "I can't thank you enough for taking the time to speak with my son. He came home a different person. For the first time he sat down and talked respectfully to his stepfather."

With a smile, Joseph responded. "It's my pleasure, Mrs. Matos, but the real success was the decision that your son made."

Joseph excused himself and walked back to the main workout area, called a dojo.

Joseph, Nick Anderson and the four police officers were standing at the head of the class.

Joseph started by addressing the class, "All right, you guys. Pull yourselves together and focus on what I am going to say."

The fourteen kids picked up their heads and focused their attention on Joseph Galardi, who continued to speak. "Every one of you has a fighting chance, and every one of you has a different gift that you can use. The question you have to ask yourself is: Are you going to use that gift to mess up this world or to better it? Every decision you make has a consequence, and you can't blame others for the decisions you make. The owner of this karate school is an awesome martial artist and teacher. For the next six months he is going to train you guys to be the best you can be. The karate part is the least important. He's going to teach you to be leaders and achievers. For many of you, the dreams you have inside will begin to show themselves. It's not going to cost you any money for these classes. However, there is one thing you need to give back in return: to pass on what you learn. Many of you are in high school, and a few of you are in the work place doing a job you hate. For those of you who are in an unpleasant job, during this time of training you may consider going to college and getting a degree. Mr. Anderson will help you by leading you in the right direction. The rest is up to you. As for all of you, these next six months will shine a new light on you, and you will be looked up to in your schools and work places. What you need to give back is the same thing you are going to receive. Being a good example and leading your friends down the right road. You will all see how important you are, and in return, you must help others realize how important they are. My desire, along with the rest of these men, is not to round up kids and place them in jail, but rather to help you become what you are capable of being. My name is Joseph Galardi, and I am a detective. We have a group of young people like yourselves back in Florida, and they are called the Fighting Chance team. As of right now, we have formed another team right here in Chicago."

The fourteen boys began to smile. For the first time they felt important.

Returning their smiles, Joseph continued. "Welcome. These four men here with Mr. Anderson and myself are Chicago detectives. They are here to help you in whatever you may need. You will be able to bring kids to this school, and they will be able to receive the same training you will.

Yesterday I told you that anyone who didn't show up here this morning would be prosecuted. As of now I am making a different rule. Your decisions are your consequences, and if you do not want to take part in what I just spoke of then you are free to leave right now. That is your decision, and a consequence will follow. Is there anyone who wishes to leave at this time?"

Joseph stopped talking and gave the opportunity to anyone who wished to take it.

After a moment, Double K got up from where he was sitting and headed toward the door. Stitch was disappointed to see him leave but didn't say anything because it was Double K's decision.

As Double K reached the door, he grabbed the already opened door and pulled on the handle, but stepped back inside as the door closed. Double K said to the group with a smile, "I thought I'd close the door since no one wants to leave. Let's get to work, I'm in."

The rest of the boys smiled, and they started clapping to show that they approved and were excited to begin.

Joseph and the four men joined in on the clapping and cheering. After a moment, Joseph gave a proper introduction to their new instructor. "Gentlemen, I would like to introduce to you a master at what he does, your new instructor: Sensei Nick Anderson. He is to be addressed as Mr. Anderson."

The boys gave another round of applause for Mr. Anderson.

Chapter
Sixteen

The Mall Competition
Is On

The Woodfield Mall competition was only one week away, there was much work to be done for both Dominique and Jonathan.

Joseph, Monica, Dominique and Josh were back at the hotel gathered around the computer and talking with Adam and the rest of the team back at the Zone.

"You just give the order, Mr. Galardi, and we'll do it," Adam said, as the rest of the team was ready to go.

"What order are you talking about?" Jackie asked, coming out of the bathroom.

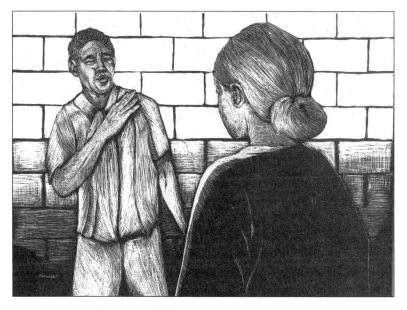

"Heaven help us! What did you do in there?" DJ said, waving his hand past his nose.

"Must have been something in those cookies I ate last night," Jackie responded, giving DJ a little push.

"Maybe it's because you ate twelve of them," Billy added.

"Yeah, that could have done it," Jackie said, seriously considering that as a possibility.

"Jackie, we're sorry we can't be there for the near death experience that you and the rest of the team are experiencing," Mr. Galardi expressed.

"It's not that bad," Jackie commented.

"Of course it's not for you, but I've got nose hairs burning over here," DJ said.

"Grow up, DJ." Kelly added as she continued. "You don't have nose hairs."

Everyone at the Zone and in Chicago began to laugh at Kelly's remark to DJ. Of course, DJ, being the kind of guy he is, laughed right along with them.

"Anyway," Mr. Galardi said, getting back to business. "Yes, Adam, on what we discussed. We are all heading outside to the back part of the hotel, so why don't you fill Jackie in on what's going on?"

"Yes, sir, Mr. Galardi," Adam responded with respect, then continued. I just hope the transport machine still works. It may malfunction due to the high content of methane gas down here in the basement of this old mill."

The rest of the team stood in shock as they heard what Adam said. They had no idea what he was talking about. Why would anything Adam invented stop working all of a sudden?

Without warning, Yuri burst out laughing. "Ah, I get it...methane gas. He's talking about the smell coming from Jackie."

No one expected Adam to make a funny or even participate on a humorous level. They all started to laugh and patted Adam on the back for coming up with a good one. Even the Chicago foursome was laughing along with them.

Adam just smiled, feeling pretty good that he actually fit in on their level. "Ha, ha. I made a funny. It wasn't that good," Adam said, as they continued to praise him.

"Hey, even I liked it, Adam," Jackie said, giving him a pat on the shoulder.

After they all enjoyed a few laughs, Mr. Galardi and the rest were heading to the back of the hotel, as Adam began to fill Jackie and the rest in on what needed to be done.

"We are going to transport Monica, Mrs. Galardi, back here to the Zone, and she is going to get the rest of her kids along with their vehicle . We are going to transport them back to Chicago."

Jackie interrupted. "How are we going to get their vehicle down here in the basement of this mill?"

"We send a transport door right to their house, silly," Adam answered. He continued, "Why are we doing this, you ask? Because our very own Dominique is going to compete in a singing competition that may lead to a recording contract," Adam said with a proud smile.

"Cool. We have a superstar working with us," Jackie said.

"All right, we're here," Mr. Galardi said, interrupting Jackie.

"We copy you, Mr. Galardi. Mrs. Galardi, we are going to call you Monica from now on, if that's OK with you. The reason is because we don't want any mix-up while we are communicating. You know the Mr./Mrs. stuff may become confusing," Adam said, as he geared up for perfection.

Monica agreed, and the Chicago group prepared for the arrival of the portable C-1 transport door. No matter how many times they saw that door come out of the ground, it was still fascinating.

Joseph, Monica, Dominique and Josh were behind the hotel. Within a few seconds the ground began to ripple. There were small bolts of lightning that struck around the rippling area, and in the blink of an eye, the C-1 door shot out of the ground and opened. A slight fog came out from inside the doors and was now ready for transport.

"Ready when you are, Monica," Adam said.

Mr. Galardi comforted her by saying, "All right, honey, don't worry. You'll be fine. Get the kids and the vehicle, and we'll see you back here in three hours."

Monica nodded her head and stepped into the C-1 door.

Mr. Galardi stepped in for a second and gave her a kiss. Then he stepped out as he said, "Don't forget to call as soon as you get back to the Zone, OK?"

Monica nodded her head, and the doors closed, as they shot back into the ground. She was off.

Mr. Galardi, Dominique and Josh just stood there for a second, staring at nothing. Mr. Galardi took a deep breath, and before he could let it out, he heard, "Honey, I'm home!" Monica comments as she continued, "I can get used to this kind of travel."

Before Joseph could even answer back, Monica sent another comment to the Chicago group. "Oh my gosh, it smells like something died in here," referring to Jackie's bathroom mishap. "No more cookies for you, girl," Monica said with a smile as she began to give the team hugs.

Back at the Karate School

The next day, Monica, the kids and the vehicle made it safely to Chicago. She was gathering things together for the day while. Dominique, Josh and her husband were at the karate school.

At the karate school, the fourteen boys had just finished their first and most intense workout ever.

Some of them were lying on the floor exhausted, while the rest just leaned against the wall.

Jonathan walked over to the stereo and put on an upbeat song. The music began to play, and five of the exhausted boys couldn't take it any longer. They jumped to their feet and began to dance.

They had been dancing together for quite some time, and the moves they were doing were fantastic.

Everyone gathered around and enjoyed watching the boys do their thing.

Just before the song finished, Jonathan turned off the music and ran over to the five boys with an exciting idea.

"Hey, check this out, you guys," Jonathan said as he continued. "I got this singing thing next week, so why don't you be the backup dancers to the song I am going to sing?"

"For real?" one of the boys asked.

"Of course, for real. So what do you say?" Jonathan repeated, waiting for an answer.

"Dude, if you're serious, we're in," one of the boys commented, speaking for the rest of them.

"Hey, what about the rest of us?" one of the other guys yelled.

"Can you dance?" Jonathan asked.

"No, not really," he answered back.

"All right, then. Let's see. How about...ah...that's it. You can watch," Jonathan replied jokingly as they all started to laugh.

Jonathan began to explain that he was going to sing, "My Girl," at the Woodfield Mall competition. The five dancers gave him a strange look as if they wondered, How in the world do you expect us to dance to that song? Jonathan saw their confusion and had an answer for that.

"I know, you think the song is too slow," Jonathan added. "All right, check this out. Right in the middle of the song there is a vocal break. That's where I throw in a rap twist to the song, and that's where you guys come out dancing. Here, let me show you."

Jonathan put the song track on and began to sing. Stitch was taken aback by Jonathan's vocals.

"Dude, this boy can sing." Stitch complimented.

Jonathan got to the part where the vocal break was and instead of just letting the music play out, that's where he began to rap. Everyone was amazed at how cool the rap fit in with the rest of the song.

As soon as the rap part was over, Jonathan stopped the music. "You guys see what I'm talking about?" Jonathan expressed.

"For sure. That's right on, man," one of the guys said in total agreement.

"You know what, though? The music needs to have a rap beat to it rather than the one that comes with the track. What do you think?" Dominique added, trying to make the song better.

"I see what you mean," Jonathan answered, not really knowing how to solve the problem.

Tailgate began to talk "I got a suggestion. It might just work." Tailgate paused for a moment and then continued,

"My brother and I have a brand-new digital mixing board in our house. Well, actually it's my father's. My father does a lot of recording for our church, and we do all the mixing. If you come over, we can lay down any beat you want and make our own track."

"You guys have all these talents, and you were willing to throw them all away on a life that leads to nowhere?" Mr. Galardi commented with a confused smile.

They all stopped talking to think for a moment. A light bulb went off in their heads. Everything seemed to click.

"We never really thought we had talent," one of the guys replied.

For the first time, they felt needed and important.

"Hey, wait a minute. If you think I can sing, you should hear Dominique. Dude, she like explodes a song," Jonathan said. Then he directed a question to Dominique. "Are you going to sing, 'Somewhere Over the Rainbow' again?"

"Yes, I am. As a matter of fact, I think the lady asked us to sing the same songs we sang the last time," Dominique answered.

"Why doesn't she just come over? We can lay down an original track for her, too. You know, one that will fit her style," Jonathan said, excited at everything that was happening.

Stitch just looked at Jonathan and didn't say a word. After a moment, Jonathan questioned his silence, "What's the matter?"

Stitch answered, completely impressed. "This is totally wild. You and Dominique are unbelievable. It seems like you care more about helping each other than winning."

Nobody said anything. It was one of those awkward moments where you just don't know what to say.

Nick walked over to Joseph Galardi and privately shook his hand. "Joseph, thank you for letting me be part of this. I would have just written them off and called the police."

Joseph responded, "It's amazing what can happen when you give someone the opportunity to express their gifts and do good. You've got to get them started, though. As you just saw, many kids don't even know they have a gift or talent. As they keep going, the rest of them will find a place to help out and feel needed as well."

"Thanks again," Nick expressed with great appreciation.

Jonathan had all the guys listening as Dominique sang her song a cappella. That means "without any music."

They were clapping and cheering, and she wasn't even finished with the song.

Everything was off to a good start.

Chapter
Seventeen

Adam's Big Breakthrough
Invention and the Big Mall Day

The sun had just come up. Adam was working hard by himself at the Zone. He had a dry-erase board filled with formulas and three computers running at the same time.

Leaving one of the computers, Adam ran over to the dry-erase board and began to write another portion to his already lengthy formula. He paused for a moment, chewed on the marker and stared at the board with great thought.

Slowly putting the marker back into the tray at the bottom of the board, he made his way back to the computers, which were still loading the programs he had just finished writing.

Adam heard the pulley-driven elevator begin to move, and he quickly turned to see who was there. He was startled because it was barely sunup. Who could be there this early in the morning? Besides, no one knew about this place except the team. Surely they were not up this early.

"Who's there?" Adam asked with great concern.

"It's me, Billy."

The elevator arrived to the basement, and Adam could see that it really was Billy.

"Oh my gosh, you scared me, Billy. I didn't expect anyone to be here this early."

Billy got off the elevator and then commented, "I had a feeling you were up to something. I thought you could use a hand. How long have you been here?"

"I never left from last night," Adam answered. Taking a deep breath, he continued, "Billy, if this works, this will be my most exciting accomplishment to date."

Billy couldn't imagine what else Adam had invented. "What is it?"

Adam focused for a moment, trying to explain in terms that Billy could understand. "You know how the transport door shoots out of the ground and stuff?"

Billy acknowledged as Adam continued. "I have been working on a transport that deals with magnetic molecules. It's like this: I have come up with a way to shock molecules with such high intensity that they become magnetic. Then I can control them."

Billy interrupted, "Hold on. Hold on. You've lost me. What does it do?"

"I can make a transport portal appear anywhere in any situation. There is no more portable transport door. It's like a circle of magnetic dust particles. The particles, at the time of departure and arrival, push to the side and there you are. No more door or anything. It's like you can appear almost out of no where."

"No way! Does it work?" Billy questioned.

"I don't know, but since you're here, let's give it a try," Adam said.

Billy took a few chairs and placed them into the C-1

transport in the basement of the Zone. He and Adam began to push buttons and do multiple jobs due to the fact that some of the other team members were not there.

Adam showed Billy how, after Adam ignited power from sector four, he must flip the switch right next to the computer pad at sector five. This would give the intense power boost that was needed to operate the new door.

"Adam, where will these chairs be transported?"

"Look right behind you," Adam commented. "Just watch. This is going to blow your mind."

Adam went through a few more checkpoints, then was ready to make this happen.

"Are you ready, Billy?"

"Let's do it," Billy replied.

The main C-1 transport door closed, and the operation was in motion.

"Ready, Billy...Now! Power to sector four, and switch on at sector five."

Billy did exactly what Adam said. There was no rumble, ripple or lightning bolts—nothing.

"Look behind you," Adam said as Billy quickly turned around.

In mid-air the magnetic molecules began to form very quickly. Within seconds the molecules pushed to the outer parts of the circle, forming a thick black line in the form of a ring. There they were: the two chairs in the middle of nowhere.

"Can we reach inside and grab them?" Billy asked, somewhat concerned.

"Absolutely," Adam replied as he went over and reached in to grab the chairs.

Adam pushed a button on his computer, and the molecules disappeared. He looked over at Billy and smiled. "It worked. Finally, it worked. Yes!" Adam rejoiced as he leaned his head back, exhausted but relieved.

A few days later, after Adam had tested the new transport portal at least thirty five times, the team was very excited and couldn't wait to use it in a real situation. Adam had tested not only his dog, but also Mr. Galardi, who had been to Florida and back.

The Day of the Big Competition

There were two thousand people at the mall and twenty-five more performers to go.

The crowd went wild as the singers performed. The stage was set with lights and smoke to give an awesome effect for each of the performers.

There was a panel of ten judges. Three of them were record producers from Hollywood recording studios, and the rest of them were agents and casting directors from both Nashville and California.

The age limit for this competition was from twelve to eighteen. The performers were both nervous and excited at the same time.

The singers at this competition were far more professional than those at the last one.

It just so happened that Dominique and Jonathan were the last two singers to take the stage.

The time had come, and it was Dominique's turn to take the stage. Her family was there with her, and they were all excited to hear her sing.

The announcer introduced Dominique to the audience, and the complimentary cheers filled the area.

She looked out at the audience and saw her family along with Jonathan and everyone from the karate school. She was not expecting to see the others: Yuri, Kelly, Jackie and DJ were cheering her on as well. She shook her head and topped it off with a huge smile as her song began.

Dominique was just a few lines into the song when the crowd began to go wild. They had not cheered like that for any of the other performers, nor had the judges heard anything like it.

The cheers continued throughout the song as Dominique built the momentum of the song. Her new version brought a different flair to the song. Tailgate and the rest of the street boys were excited far beyond how the crowd was responding.

As the song came to an end the audience was at a fever pitch. It was clear that no other performer had come even close to Dominique's level of performance today.

The crowd did not stop cheering, even to the point where the announcer couldn't be heard to introduce Jonathan.

Finally the crowd settled. The announcer introduced Jonathan and brought him to the stage. Again the crowd gave a complimentary cheer, but the karate school kids and the Galardi family applauded above and beyond for Jonathan.

Stepping onto the stage, Jonathan looked calm and ready to give his best. He looked out into the audience and saw his mother and brothers smiling at him. When he saw his father smiling, his heart was overwhelmed with joy— a joy he had never experienced from his father before.

His song, "My Girl," began, and Jonathan started to move a little with the music. As he began to sing the crowd was floored by Jonathan's voice, but not nearly as much as his father Nick, who had never really seen him perform live before today.

Jonathan was doing far better than the other performers of the day but had not reached the level that Dominique had attained.

Jonathan was right in the middle of the song when the vocal break began. That's where the new version of the song was added. The rap beat began, and the dancers made it onto the stage. Their moves were unbelievable, and Jonathan joined them. The crowd was screaming, just like they were with Dominique. This was the first time today that anyone had used dancers.

The dancing and the singing continued all the way to the end of the song.

Nick couldn't believe what he was seeing and hearing. His son was fabulous, and the crowd was going crazy.

As the song ended the crowd was going wild, just as they did for Dominique.

The announcer made his way to the stage and addressed the crowd. "Wow! Where did those two acts just come from?"

The crowd began to cheer all over again, and the announcer had to calm them down before he could continue. "The judges are adding up all the votes, and we will have our winner in just a few moments. To let you know how the voting works, each judge places a number from one to ten, one being least and ten being best, on their voter's card. Each performer has a card, and each judge has a card. The performer with the most points gathered from all the judges is our winner. Since this competition is looking for a winner to compete in the national competition, there will be no second or third place winners."

The announcer continued talking to the crowd about various high points in the competition as Nick and his two sons Mike and Kevin couldn't believe what they just heard.

"If you boys would not have been so headstrong that he had to be the karate men like you all are then you would have seen his singing talents much earlier," Jonathan's mom, Linda, said to her two boys and her husband, Nick.

Nick put his arm around his wife and gave her a kiss on the forehead. "Thanks for being patient with me and for being there for Jonathan when I wasn't."

Nick and Linda just looked at each other and smiled. This had been quite an eye opener for everyone.

The Anderson family moment was broken when they heard the announcer begin to talk about the winner.

"Ladies and gentlemen! May I have your attention, please," The announcer said. "We have had a day of extraordinary performers and performances, but not everyone can win today. This doesn't mean you should stop following your dreams. To have made it this far should tell you something. Can we give a nice round of applause to all of our performers here today?"

The crowd gave a short burst of cheer. They didn't want to stretch it out too long because they were waiting to hear who the winner was.

The announcer had the winning card in his hand and began to address the crowd once more. "At this time I would like to bring back to the stage the top two performers. From there we will announce our first place winner. Are you ready?"

The crowd let out another cheer.

The announcer continued, "In no specific order I would like to bring back to the stage Mr. Jonathan Anderson and Miss Dominique Galardi."

The crowd cheered out of control. It was obvious that the two picked were their favorites as well.

Jonathan and Dominique made their way to the stage and the cheers continued.

The announcer began talking to both of them. "The performances that came from you have been the very best we have seen in this competition yet."

The crowd cheered again, and Dominique and Jonathan humbly thanked the announcer for his kind comments.

"Let's see who the winner is," The announcer said as he opened the envelope that was given to him by one of the judges.

The moment was very tense, and the crowd was waiting with great anticipation.

The announcer continued, "I don't believe this. We have a tie. The judges will cast their vote once more, and then there will be a final decision."

The place was going wild, and the tension continued to build.

The judge handed the announcer another envelope with the final vote.

Before he opened it he excited the crowd once more. "The winner of this competition will not only walk away with one thousand dollars but will also go on to compete in the national competition where first place is a recording contract."

Opening the envelope for the second time the announcer pulled out the voter's card and addresses the crowd. "This vote is final, and you won't believe this, but it's another tie."

The crowd was going out of control again because they liked both of the singers, and they were glad to see them both win.

Dominique and Jonathan hugged each other. The excitement was overwhelming for Jonathan, and he had tears rolling down his face.

Nick and the rest of Jonathan's family made their way to the stage to congratulate Jonathan. The Galardi's and the Fighting Chance team were on their way as well to congratulate Dominique.

Jonathan was still hugging Dominique when he felt a tap on his shoulder. He turned to see his father and lunged toward him with a hug as the tears were streaming down both of their cheeks.

The Galardi family was hugging and kissing Dominique and the crowd is still cheering.

After a moment the cheering calmed down so the announcer could explain what had to happen. "Congratulations to both of you. Your talents are magnificent. Because of the tie you will split the one thousand dollars, but the good news is that both of you will be competing in the national competition for the first place position and the recording contract."

The crowd began to cheer once more, and the judges stood to their feet, applauding along with the crowd.

Chapter Eighteen

What's Next?

Jackie, Yuri, Kelly and DJ were transported back to the Zone right after the competition finished.

It was the day after the big event, and everyone was gathered at the karate school. Nick honored his son well. He threw a party right in the middle of the school to celebrate the two winners.

Many of the students who were at the party saw the mall competition on the news and were getting autographs from both Dominique and Jonathan.

Jonathan felt a great sense of accomplishment, and most of all, his father is proud of him.

Over in the corner of the room Jonathan and Dominique were chatting with their fourteen new friends. They were brainstorming ideas for the next big event: the national competition.

They were enjoying their big moment of glory. The good thing about all of this was that Jonathan made the fourteen kids feel like they were part of his big win by using the dancers and involving Tailgate in the remix of the song he sang.

One of the fourteen made his way toward Dominique to congratulate her on the awesome job she did. His name was Tommy.

"Your voice blew me away, Dominique," Tommy commented with a smile.

"Thank you. I'm glad you enjoyed the song," Dominique answered.

"I was wandering if you would like to go to a movie with me or something like that?" Tommy asked in a shy way.

"Ah, that was very nice of you to ask, but my father doesn't allow me to date," Dominique replied back.

Jonathan was watching the whole thing because he liked Dominique and was waiting to see what she would say. When she gave Tommy her answer, he smiled with a sigh of relief.

"Are you cool with that, that your father doesn't let you date?" Tommy asked.

"Very cool," Dominique responded. She continued, "He explained how important relationships can be and how so many young people get hurt because they don't know what they are getting themselves into. My dad's real cool. All my friends like him, and my girlfriends don't date either because of what he said. When the right person comes along, we'll take it from there."

"Maybe we can just be friends then," Tommy said as he extended his hand.

"We can definitely be friends," Dominique responded as she shook his hand.

Tommy walked away, and Dominique heard someone

talking to her from behind. "What about me?" Jonathan asked. "Are you going to be my friend, too?"

Dominique turned to see who it was. Once she saw that it was Jonathan, she gave him a great big hug. "You were awesome today. The very best to the both of us. I'm hoping one of us walks away with that big win."

"Maybe it will be another tie," Jonathan said in a serious way.

"Not this time. The judges told me, only one."

Mr. Galardi came up from behind the two of them and put his arms around them both. "I'm so proud of you two. Your performances were absolutely brilliant."

Dominique and Jonathan just smiled, not really knowing what to say.

"Don't forget what I told you," Mr. Galardi said to Jonathan.

"You told me a lot. Which part would you like me to remember?" Jonathan added with a smile.

"The part when I said, if others don't believe in you that's OK, but if you stop believing in you it's over." Mr. Galardi said.

"Oh yeah, that part. Don't worry, I'll never forget that," Jonathan replied as he extended his hand to shake and seal the deal.

"C'mon, Dominique. We have to get going," her dad said to her.

Both Dominique and her dad walked toward Monica and the rest of their family. Nick and his wife were talking to Monica, and Joseph jumped in on the conversation. "Well, Nick, thank you for taking care of me when I didn't know who 'me' was."

They all laughed as Nick responded to that. "You've been a great blessing to our family and to my boy. We're going to miss you. But we're going to see a lot of you here in Chicago, aren't we?"

"We will definitely be in touch, and I'll see you in California for the National Singing competition," Joseph said as he shook hands with Nick.

Back at the Zone

The entire Fighting Chance team was at the Zone, awaiting Adam's orders to bring the Galardi family back home.

Adam and DJ were having a conversation about the amount of magnetic energy it would take to operate the new transport door. Billy was sitting at his station, gearing up the computer for the arrivals.

Kelly approached Billy and asked, "Hey, Billy. Did you see where I put my portable computer?"

Billy looked up and answered, "Yes, I did see it." He looked around and then realized he had moved it to the table behind him. He got up to get it. "I put it on this table. I'll get it for you." Billy handed her the portable computer.

"Thank you, Billy," Kelly said. "You can be very cute when you're not acting like a dork."

"Thank you, I think," Billy replied.

"You're welcome." She added, "But don't get any ideas. I'm taking Mr. Galardi's advice on relationships."

"Me, too," Billy agreed.

Adam interrupted the team. "The boss is ready. Let's do it."

The team manned their positions, and the transport process began.

"Mr. Galardi, we are going to send the portable door. Are you ready?"

"Ready, Adam," Mr. Galardi said, then gave the signal.

Suddenly the emergency indicator went off at the Zone.

"Hold on, Mr. Galardi, we have an emergency coming in," Adam said, as he continued to view the readout.

"Mr. Galardi, we have an emergency. There's a mother and her sixteen-year-old daughter trapped on the seventeenth floor of their apartment building. Floors thirteen through nineteen are completely engulfed in fire. Everyone else is out, and the rescue team cannot get to them. They are going to die, Mr. Galardi, if we don't get to them quickly. The building is collapsing around them!"

"What do I need to do?" Mr. Galardi asked with great concern.

"I can put you right in their living room with our new transport door. You can grab them and bring them in with you, and I will transport you right behind the building to a safe spot. We need to make a decision right now. You'll be in and out before you can take a deep breath."

Joseph looked at his wife, and they both looked at their daughter, imagining if it were them in that situation. She gave him a nod of confirmation.

"Let's do it, Adam," Mr. Galardi says.

Adam took control of the operation. "Hang tight,

Galardi family. I'll have the boss back in just a minute. Josh, fire up the laptop, and you guys can watch all this from the hotel room. Mr. Galardi, we need to see you. Reach in your bag and pull out the clear, flat, two-inch piece of plastic. Hold it to your forehead for three seconds, and it will stick without falling off. I know it works in intense heat. I put it in my mother's oven to watch biscuits cook once."

Joseph did what Adam asked. Adam gave it a quick check, and it was working perfectly. Mr. Galardi was ready to go.

Within seconds, the magnetic circle, also called the transport portal, appeared right there in the hotel room. It opened, and Mr. Galardi stepped in. It was gone in a flash. They all gathered around the laptop to watch what was happening via transmission from the Zone.

Joseph Galardi arrived precisely where Adam said he would. However, when he stepped out of the portal the room was quickly filling with smoke. There was fire all around him.

He looked over to the sofa and found the mother and daughter barely conscious.

"Adam, I see them. Leave the portal open, I'm going after them."

"Yes, sir, I read you loud and clear, sir," Adam responded.

Just as Adam spoke, there was a crash. A piece of the ceiling collapsed right in front of the portal door.

"Adam, the ceiling collapsed! I can't get to the door. The fire is building. Hurry, Adam, relocate the door!"

"There's no where for it to transport," Adam answered.

There was a build up of pressure inside the room, and Adam heard an explosion.

"What was that?" Adam called out.

"I don't know. It could be anything, and another part of the ceiling has collapsed. Adam, the smoke is increasing. I need an answer quickly!" Mr. Galardi cried out in great concern for his life and the lives of the mother and daughter.

Monica and the Chicago group were trying to stay calm. Monica instructed the two smaller children to watch the television so they couldn't see what was happening from the images on the laptop.

Back at the Zone the entire team was concentrating so intensely that the sweat showed on their faces.

"Adam, I need an answer, now!" Mr. Galardi screamed.

THE END

Will Mr. Galardi escape from the fire?
How?

Will either Dominique or Jonathan make it to the top
three finalists in the national singing competition?
If so, what will happen?

Get ready for
A FIGHTING CHANCE
BOOK 3

Jonathan Charles Vaughan

Born in London, England, Vaughan began to make art at an early age. Spending afternoons water coloring with his father both from nature and photographs, art making quickly became a favorite activity. In 1985, his family immigrated to Florida and since that time he has lived in a number of states before returning back to Orlando in 2002.

He received his Bachelors of Fine Arts Degree in the Fine Arts from The School of Visual Arts in New York City and his Masters of Arts in Teaching the Visual Arts Degree from The University of the Arts in Philadelphia. Currently, he is an art instructor for Seminole Community College in Sanford, Florida and a substitute teacher for Seminole County Public School System based in Lake Mary, Florida.

His list of exhibitions includes shows at The University of the Arts in Philadelphia, The School of Visual Arts in Savannah, The Downtown Branch of the Orange County Library System in Orlando, and The First Thursday Event at the Orlando Museum of Art.

His awards include a Best of Show ribbon from the City of Orlando's Fine Arts Fair in 1999, The Sylvia G. Wexler Memorial Award for Art Education from The University of the Arts, and a purchase award from Valencia Community College in Orlando.

This book holds his first published illustrations and he hopes the you enjoy looking at them as much as he enjoyed making them.

My name is Thomas Inman. I am currently a fourth-grader at Deerwood Elementary in Orlando, Florida. I enjoy school, reading, baseball and video games. Winning "THE FIGHTING CHANCE" essay contest was the coolest thing to ever happen to me!